The Ivory Trail

The Ivory Trail

T.V. Bulpin

PROTEA BOOK HOUSE
Pretoria
2011

The Ivory Trail
T.V. Bulpin

First edition, first impression in 1954 by Howard Timmins
Second edition, first impression in 1967 by Books of Africa
Third edition, first impression in 1982 by Books of Africa
Fourth edition, first impression in 2011 by Protea Book House

PO Box 35110, Menlo Park, 0102
1067 Burnett Street, Hatfield, Pretoria
8 Minni Street, Clydesdale, Pretoria
protea@intekom.co.za
www.proteaboekhuis.com

Editor: Danél Hanekom
Proofreader: Amelia de Vaal
Cover design: Hanli Deysel
Front cover image: Louis Smit
Illustrations: C.T. Astley Maberly
Typography: 11 on 14 pt Zapf Calligraphic by Ada Radford
Printed and bound: Paarlmedia, Paarl

© 2011 M.M.M. Bulpin
ISBN: 978-1-86919-464-2

Contents

The old Ivory Trail 1903-1929

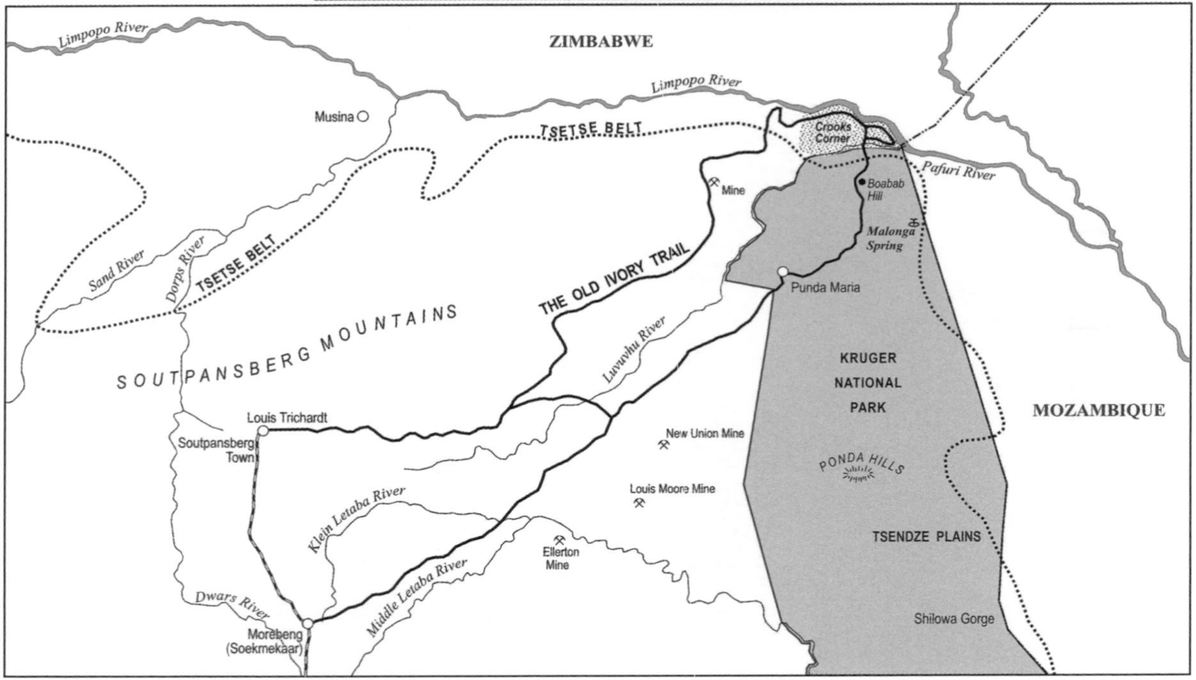

ZIMBABWE

MOZAMBIQUE

Limpopo River

Pafuri River

Crooks Corner

Baobab Hill

Malonga Spring

Punda Maria

KRUGER NATIONAL PARK

PONDA HILLS

TSENDZE PLAINS

Shilowa Gorge

Mine

THE OLD IVORY TRAIL

T.S.E.T.S.E. BELT

TSETSE BELT

Luvuvhu River

New Union Mine

Louis Moore Mine

Ellerton Mine

Musina

Limpopo River

Dorps River

Sand River

S O U T P A N S B E R G   M O U N T A I N S

Klein Letaba River

Middle Letaba River

Louis Trichardt

Soutpansberg Town

Dwars River

Moræleng (Soekmekaar)

Prelude

I don't know exactly when it was that I first heard of Bvekenya. It was at some campfire, out in the bush. We were lounging around after a hard, hot day: some of the chaps were half asleep, some cleaning their rifles, some just lying against a tree-trunk, reflecting in lazy pleasure over the beans and sausages, while the dogs sat on their haunches, still panting every time they remembered the day's pursuits, their tongues hanging red in the firelight.

It was at one of these evening camps that somebody mentioned Bvekenya. I remember my first half-interest. "*Bvekenya*? Odd sort of name – *The one who swaggers as he walks*. Why did the Shanganes call him that?" Nobody knew. They knew, instead, all manner of legends and tales about him. Indeed, in a casual way, I learned much of Bvekenya in the months that followed. Whenever someone told a yarn of the bush, somehow or other Bvekenya entered it. Nobody knew his real name, where he had come from, or whether he was dead. He was a legend of the bush; and as the bush is secret and ageless, so its legends come from all ages, mix themselves up irrespective of years, and go on to the future like a trail whose beginnings are tree-grown and whose makers have vanished completely.

It was not only the Europeans who remembered Bvekenya. The Shangane tribespeople knew him well. They too had their stories about him. They talked to me at the fires sometimes, while I lay back and chewed on some sinewy biltong. They told me their own legends about a legendary character: of beatings and shootings and fightings; of how he had hunted and killed both man and beast; and how, too, he had helped and aided and saved from starvation. A curious confliction of stories of a man, half ogre, half saviour.

So it happened that one June night I was in a camp by the banks of the Limpopo. It was a cool evening that tempted one to accept the African mythology of the night, that darkness is but the blanket of the sun. Each night he draws the blanket over himself when he goes to rest; but because it is so old it is full of moth holes, and so the stars come shining through.

The river seemed as languid as the night. The Limpopo normally is a sulky, erratic sort of river, full of sudden violence, wearing itself out in mighty floods and then relapsing from rage to a sullen brooding in the captivity of its banks.

I was alone in the camp with a few Shanganes. The night was still young. It seemed only an hour ago that *Maphungubwe* (the jackal) had first sung his paean in praise of the darkness, and over all the African world there seemed to lie an expectant silence. It was as though the birds and beasts were all intently listening, waiting for some creature bolder than the rest to sound the first note in that curious symphony of sounds which is the melody of the African night.

I sat in the camp and listened to the stillness. I wondered what lay hidden beyond the darkness, what sounds were smothered by that blanket of quiet. Out there beyond that baobab, among the hills, surely the lions had already made their kill; and in those heights the leopards must long since have stirred from such comforts as a cold lair offered, and were roaming out with eager claw and silent pad to make the shadows dangerous and give the darkness eyes.

Thus it was that I remembered the story fragments of past nights, and while I considered them and fitted them together like the pieces of a jigsaw puzzle, I first met Bvekenya.

He was five feet ten inches tall and as rugged as a buffalo. I looked up from the embers and my dreams and saw him standing in the half-shadows beyond the fire, where the light wrestles to drive back the night.

"Hello," he said casually, and walked closer with the softness of a cat.

I stared at him.

"The name's Barnard," he said. "Cecil Barnard. Most people call me Bvekenya."

I stood up and went to meet him. We shook hands and I told him who I was.

"I seem to have known you for years," I said. "I've heard more about you in these parts than I can remember."

He grunted and sat down.

"Good or bad stories?" he enquired without much concern.

"Middling," I replied. "A mixture of both."

He grunted again.

"Well, that's the way it is," he said. "A good mixture, good and bad. There's no denying it."

We looked at each other across the fire.

"Smoke?" I asked, "Or drink?"

He shook his head. "Don't do either," he said, "and if you ask me what I do, I'll tell you that there are a lot more interesting things in life. If you don't know about them you must be pretty slow."

I agreed with him, and threw over a chunk of biltong and a knife. He whittled off a sizable supply.

There was the quality in the night which made the fire companionable.

He swatted a mosquito expertly and seemed at ease.

"Where are you from?" I asked.

"Just beyond the trees," he replied, "visiting old places."

"Bringing back memories?"

He nodded.

"Plenty. It's been some time since I was last here."

"When was the first time?" I asked hopefully.

The night was young, the fire lively: for an African night's entertainment the setting was ideal. He reflected in silence for a while. Some nightbird, wandering through the velvet of the sky, sent an eerie call whimpering down from the heights.

"It's funny how these things start," he said at last. "I often used to wonder how I'd ever got myself here in the old days. It was fine sometimes; but often life wasn't worth it. Then I used to do some hard thinking and try to pin the blame on someone or something in the past for having got me here at all."

"Well, how did it start?" I persisted. "Where did you come from? There has to be a beginning."

He nodded.

I had no more to say. Bvekenya then (and at a dozen and more camps in all the time I was with him) told me his story, and the story of those in whose wild company he lived. He told me of his life and adventures, of the game animals he had met, of the hunts when he had tracked them down, and of times when they had tracked him; of the toughs and adventurers of his time, and of the bush and its secrets. All I have done is set the stories down and make them clearer for those who know not the wilderness, or the ways of its men and the nature of their lives.

ONE

The ivory trail

It was at the pleasant little port of Knysna, where the Indian Ocean meets the shores of Southern Africa, that Bvekenya first heard of elephants and the ivory trail. On a farm, just outside the village, he was born on 19 September 1886; and from the time he first learned to understand speech he heard stories of the elephants roaming the trails through the dark green forests that lift their arms to the heavens just inland from the tranquil little port.

To be born at Knysna was a pleasant enough start for anyone. The village has ever been a gentle, drowsy sort of place: a scattering of houses gathered around a spacious lagoon, like a good-humoured crowd waiting to welcome a ship. As few ships have ever called, the crowd has waited there a long time. The houses have grown trees to shelter themselves, like ladies opening parasols. In the cool shade they drowse in peace, while the beautiful forest stretches off and far away, with many a thicket and shadowy glade, to the mountains known as Tzitzikama.

Bvenkenya's father was of Scots descent, and his mother of mixed Dutch-Irish origin. To their international issue they gave the name of Stephanus Cecil Rutgert Barnard; and he was the fifth child of a union which was productive of nine sons and daughters.

The Barnard family were people of no small account in the Knysna area. Their home was noted for its hospitality; and innumerable were the visitors who stayed there and yarned in the evenings with old grandfather Barnard about the elephants of the Knysna forests.

For long ages, giant elephants had been as famous a feature of the district as its mammoth yellowwood and stinkwood trees. Hunting the elephants was an attraction which had brought many visitors to the forests; and for years the Barnard family had been renowned as both hosts and guides to all those persons whose greatest desire in life was to bring one of the animal monarchs of the Knysna forests crashing to its knees.

The elephants of the Knysna forests were not numerous. They had been hunted for so many years that only the most sagacious remnants of the herd still survived; but they were renowned among hunters for their exceptional size, and the difficulty of tracking them down in a forest as immense and ancient as that of Knysna.

In such an environment, then, it was inevitable that Cecil Barnard grew to boyhood with a profound impression of elephants. Hunters' stories of hairbreadth escapes and almost incredible adventures were his normal bedtime portion; and in his dreams he saw himself on the ivory trail, in search of the fortune and the excitement which he supposed to be the normal daily life of the elephant hunters.

He listened avidly to all those romantic yarns of fortunes made from giant tuskers, of the romance of the age-old ivory trade, and of the prowess and daring of the professional hunters. He heard, too, strange stories of the wisdom, strength and ferocity of the elephants, and of that legendary hunters' pot at the rainbow's end – the elephants' graveyard, where all old tuskers are said to go to die. In that fabulous cemetery they are said to leave their bones and ivory in a secret pile, whose whereabouts has eluded countless eager adventurers who have followed the ivory trail, reaching out their hands to grasp the illusionary prize, but at its end finding their fingers closing over nought save the empty sky.

Bvekenya's father, in his way, was one of those whose fingers were destined to clutch only the empty sky. Attracted by the cheap land and great markets in Paul Kruger's South African Republic in the Transvaal, where the Witwatersrand was booming and towns were springing up like mushrooms in the night, he sold his Knysna farm and removed with his family into the Republic, to new land on its western border.

A greater scenic change could scarcely have been managed in Southern Africa. From the well-watered mountains and always green fertility of Knysna, Bvekenya found himself transported to a segment of the earth which was as flat as a table-top from one horizon to the other. Within a hundred miles to the west lay the Kalahari desert; and although the farm of his parents' choice enjoyed some rainfall, the proximity of the thirstland was an eternal threat. Each sunset was a blaze of reds and oranges and yellows: a warning that beyond the horizon's rim lay the agony of a land without water, where the sun, sinking to expected rest, had burned the wilderness into sterility and deformed the bush into twisted, drought-resisting shrubs.

The land of the new farm, Kaalplaas, near Schweizer-Reneke, was productive and good. It was new land and cheap; and that, indeed, had been the initial attraction. Old Barnard had sold his Knysna home to raise capital for a fresh start, on a pioneer farm whose purchase would still leave him with money enough to develop and work it.

A year of hard work passed. The farm was slowly changing. It was being moulded and shaped, almost imperceptibly, to the planning of old Barnard. He had big hopes for this new home of his. He laboured with his sons all day; and certainly if human effort and perspiration could fertilize a farm, that place would have flourished amazingly.

Bvekenya was a suntanned youngster of ten years when disaster came. He was returning to the homestead with his father one evening, dusty and weary from a day of ploughing. The two paused a while, as farmers do, to appraise their stock as they passed their herd of cattle. It was old Barnard's delight to point out to his sons such praiseworthy features as the animals possessed; but in those times there was additional cause for careful study of each animal every day.

For months the dread stock disease, rinderpest, had been sweeping down through the northern bush. The farmers in the south had watched its progress with numb bewilderment. As a pest it was completely unknown. There was no cure, and death alone arrested its progress. Every farmer and community could only hope that the scourge would pass them by; eating up their neighbours' stock, but by the grace of Providence leaving their own unscathed.

On this afternoon in 1896 old Barnard and his son paused on their homeward journey, and with anxious attention watched their stock. They were fine, healthy beasts, a pride to any farmer. They were all there, except one. Barnard counted the stock, counted again, and then diverted the homeward journey in order to find the missing beast.

The search was not long. They found the animal in the shade of a thorn bush. It was already far gone: a great, hulking ox that could have pulled the farmhouse down; but now it was incapable of standing and could only look at its master in misery. Barnard and his son stood in silence and watched it.

To the peasant farmer in Africa, white or black, cattle are his savings, his riches and his bank. Knowing this, then, we forgive old man Barnard for sitting down beside his ox and weeping.

The Barnards lost all their livestock. They struggled on, their faith pinned on the star of agriculture, for three more years. Then came the ultimate disaster. Again it was on an afternoon, while the family were still at work, that a horseman clattered up to the homestead.

"Good afternoon to you, Mrs Barnard," said the rider, wiping the dust from his eyes. "Where is your man?"

She told him of her husband's whereabouts and, declining the usual coffee, he cantered off.

Presently Barnard walked into the homestead. His wife had sensed the trouble already.

"It's war?"

He nodded. There was little sense in further discussion. Night after night, for months, they had talked the matter over before they slept. Such rumours, and occasional newspapers which filtered through the scattered and isolated community, had long since warned them that trouble was brewing over the riches of the Witwatersrand.

The Jameson Raid, the endless propaganda and provocation of rival mischief-makers on the Rand, had made rumours of war between the Republic and Britain a topic of conjecture for two years.

Barnard had got on well with the republicans. They were a homely company of farmers: kindly and childishly naïve at times, with the cultural standard and characteristics of peasants all over the world except that these Transvalers were unique in being probably the largest land-owning specimens of their class that history has ever known.

As a resident in the Republic, Barnard was subject to compulsory service in time of war. If he refused, the only alternative was expulsion – an even more disastrous prospect than national service. At least, as a member of the republican force, his family's home was assured. In any case, he was not unsympathetic towards the Republic's struggle to defend its independence; and neither he nor his wife had any particular regard for the international crowd of mine-owners who were considered by the Republic to be the principal instigators of the trouble.

Accordingly, Barnard rode off to do his duty for the Republic; and shortly afterwards, in 1901, became a prisoner of war. Behind him, on the farm, life had become a dreary struggle. The four older children had left with their father: some to fight, others in the hope of earning money. On the farm, Mrs Barnard and the five younger children, headed by Bvekenya, were toiling to keep the place together and make some sort of a living for themselves.

It was a dreary existence. Hardly any real news ever filtered back to the farm about the war or the fate of the fighting members of the family. Occasionally some neighbour, returning from the front wounded or on leave, would call in with some message. The only consolation for Mrs Barnard was that at least her family was not divided on the issue of the war. Some families were in the predicament of having members fighting on both sides; with feelings running so high that sons would threaten fathers in newspaper notices, saying that they would shoot their parents out of hand if they chanced to take them prisoner.

The constant worry and labour broke Mrs Barnard. In 1902, while the war was in its last convulsive stages, she sickened and died, leaving fifteen-year-old Bvekenya as the acting head of the family. To try to work the farm with his scanty knowledge and with the aid only of four younger brothers and sisters was impossible. Bvekenya had to go out and work, taking on any odd jobs an impoverished but sympathetic neighbourhood could offer, and spending most of his time transport riding.

At the end of the war things improved for Bvekenya. His father returned and relieved him from the crushing responsibility of caring for the family. He found himself, in his late teens, free to do as he pleased. His assets were few: good health, toughness, patience, and no illusions about life. His handicaps were many: a scrappy education, no family influence or associations in the outside world, and no money. What were his chances in a country still stunned by the catastrophe of war? With this bleak prospect, he packed his few clothes and on 3 April 1906, left home in search of fortune.

For a few months Bvekenya wandered around the south-western Transvaal and Orange Free State, in search of some employment. Nothing was offered him, save the pittance of a farm labourer. With his resources at an end, he at last joined the newly mustered South African Constabulary; and for three years, in Johannesburg and Standerton, he went through the enjoyable process of being knocked into parade-ground shape by British sergeant-majors and disciplined by Dutch martinets on uniformity and polish.

At this time his thoughts turned with longing to the freedom of the wilderness. The old stories of his Knysna days, of fortunes in ivory and the excitement of the elephant hunt, emerged from the half-forgotten past. The years had clothed these stories in additional garments of romance. More and more, the idea of a hunter's life appealed to him as a way of combining escape from his present discipline with a chance of fortune.

Bvekenya's police pay was meagre; but he had no extravagancies, if only because he could not afford them. At the end of his three years' probationary training period, he had a small amount of money stowed away in a savings account. He left the police, with as much regret as a bird escaping from its cage.

The cage, for those who liked it, was certainly snug and secure, with ample bodily comforts. Bvekenya saw not the consolations, but rather the confines of the policeman's way of life. To him the only future seemed to lie in a small door marked "Pensions", and to have old age as his only ambition was not to the liking of Bvekenya.

Bvekenya had never met the type of professional hunter which he longed to become. The sportsmen he had met in Knysna were mostly the moneyed amateurs, who shot to while away their leisure, and often dressed in a fashion both extravagant and silly. Influenced by them, Bvekenya had long visualised himself in the role of a great white hunter, and he made his purchases of costume and equipment along the lines indicated to him by a combination of his imagination and memory of the amateur hunters of the past.

The bulk of his savings was spent in the purchase of clothing, food, camp gear, a wagon, ten donkeys, a mule and a couple of guns, with a .303 as his best weapon. With these treasures stowed away in his wagon, he left Pretoria in the early winter of 1910, and followed that Great North Road, which has taken so many others on the first stage of some venture into the interior, yielding in the end success, or death, or bitter disappointment; but never yet failing to provide all those who have followed it for adventure's sake alone with everything, and more, that a wanderer's heart desires.

TWO

Crooks Corner

Where the Luvuvhu River twists its way through the wilderness to join the great Limpopo, there lies a forgotten corner of the Transvaal, left all alone to brood in the solitude and the silence of the bush. At the junction of the rivers this isolated wedge of land tapers off to a point: a bush-covered cape washed by the swirling waters, an old resting place of crocodiles, with a shady little beach where many an evil dream has been spun in the secret thoughts of those cruel reptiles.

Crooks Corner is the name man gave long ago to this secluded and sinister wedge of land. It was a last home for many a curious and lawless character: a sanctuary from civilisation, whose solitary state was paradise to all those whose deeds or inclinations made imperative a retreat to some last stronghold of the lawless.

This odd corner of the land had a capital: a sort of centre for the community of scallywags and adventurers and wanderers to use as their address, while their homes and happy hunting grounds were hidden somewhere deep in the impenetrable thickets of the surrounding bush.

This capital of Crooks Corner lay atop a 500-feet-high ridge, which formed a sort of topographical backbone to this wedge of land between the rivers. To the Shangane tribespeople who lived scattered sparsely in the bush the ridge was known as *Sesengamabwene* (the place of sandstone) for it was there that the huntsmen found the stones they used in braying and dressing skins. To the Europeans, however, the capital of Crooks Corner (a diminutive, non-descript little store) was known as *Makhuleke*, the name of the Shangane chief on whose lands the establishment had been erected.

Alec Thompson and William Pye had built the store of Makhuleke in the early months of 1910. It was never much of a place: just a tiny, corrugated-iron shack, falling down almost from the time it was built, its veranda leaning over drunkenly, its guttering broken.

In its time the store at Makhuleke was a bustling place, with perhaps a hundred Africans and two dozen European adventurers coming in on a single day, trading ivory and the spoil of their hunts across its battered counters for food, clothes, strong liquor, and ammunition. But the glory of Makhuleke (if it ever had any) has long since departed. The little store still stands on top of the ridge, looking wistfully out over miles of bush and solitude. The adventurers have gone, and only the local tribespeople are left to make their way up the ridge to trade.

Business is bad at Makhuleke today, and stocks are scanty. One young African manages the place for an African owner. The windowless store just bakes in the heat, its door wide open, gasping for breath, while its manager lounges in the shade outside strumming a guitar, waiting for customers, with no other sound through the long day save the soughing of the wind and the sighing of the little shop as it yearns to reach the trees where its manager drowses.

From Makhuleke an old road twists through the miles of bush and links the place with civilisation. It was along this road, in the winter of 1910, that Bvekenya first found his way with his wagon, mule and donkeys.

It was a rough sort of road, really just the scar of passing wagon wheels. Of milestones and signposts it had none; but instead, its twisting undulations through the bush were beaconed with the memories of all the adventures which had taken place along that wanderers' way in years gone by, each well remembered in the yarns and thoughts of countless people.

To Bvekenya, this road with all its roughness was like a pathway to the stars. From the moment his feet first trod upon it, with the wilderness before him and civilisation left far behind, he felt all the keen contentment and lively interest in his surroundings of a wanderer returning home from a far country.

The old adventurers' way to Makhuleke left the Great North Road at Soekmekaar, midway between the then railhead at Pietersberg and Louis Trichardt. It dropped down into the bushveld, and for some fifty miles made a thirsty journey through the heat and dust to what was known as Klein Letaba. Klein Letaba was a major milestone along this ivory trail. It was there that a disreputable old character, known to all and sundry as De Fon Siku, had a wayside hotel and carried on a trade (roaring in more ways than one) with the passing adventurers and the rough crowd of miners from the lonely bushveld mines such as the Birthday, Louis Moore, and Golden Ophir. Each Saturday they banked their wages in his bar.

Beyond the hotel at Klein Letaba, the ivory trail went eastwards to a solitary store standing at the headwaters of the *Shingwidzi* (the place of ironstone), where the wild sour-date palms grow, with their graceful boughs and dark green thickets. This store was a landmark to all travellers along the ivory trail. It marked the boundary of the lion country. From thence eastwards, all travellers proceeded with increased caution and made their journeys by daylight alone, sleeping secure in encampments made of thornbush each night.

The trail passed through its increased perils to a spring-let known as Mthomene. At that place, in the shade of the evergreen *mthoma* (ebony) trees, the adventurers found pleasant rest, sheltered from the sun and rain alike by their giant boughs.

The ivory trail, in its fifty miles of travel from the hotel at Klein Letaba, passed but few human habitations. Scattered in the bush were some isolated Shangane tribespeople, but their huts were sparse and hidden in the wilds as carefully as thoughts in a furtive mind.

Beyond Mthomene, however, ten miles eastwards into the blue, on the slopes of the bushy hillock where Punda Malia stands today, there lived a Shangane character known as Sikokololo, at a small oasis in the wilds. At this place, *Dimbye ra Sikokololo* (the fertile place of Sikokololo), all travellers paused to rest a while and hear such gossip and rumours of the ivory trail as a lively and intelligent Shangane could impart.

Sikokololo was a short, brownish-coloured old man when Bvekenya met him. He had fine gardens at this fertile place, but they gave him more trouble than contentment. He spent his life in endless bitter warfare with the wild animals over the never settled question of who was to reap his crops.

All around his gardens Sikokololo had erected with prodigious labour a vast protective fence of thorns. Around this African battlement the wild animals laid permanent siege. Within it, old Sikokololo marshalled his defences with cunning and patience. His womenfolk beat drums all night when the crops were ripening, and the place was littered with so many snares and traps that Sikokololo himself, when leaving his hut one moonless night, had come to grief in a pitfall and remained tangled in his own contrivances until morning.

To Bvekenya, Sikokololo was an ingenious and loquacious friend. The old Shangane had been involved in elephant hunting for as long as he could remember. Way back in his young days, about 1870 or earlier, he had journeyed down to Natal with a party of ivory traders. At Pietermaritzburg he had first tasted the juicy fruit of *mudoro* (the prickly pear). He acquired such a liking for this fruit that he carefully carried some of the leaves all the way back to his own retreat. There he planted them so liberally that relics of his plantation are still scattered in the northern Transvaal bush. They are the delight of countless well-filled bushpigs, warthogs and porcupines and have found their way to many a distant farmhouse, when wanderers such as Bvekenya carried leaves homewards for themselves long afterwards.

From Sikokololo's fortified gardens the ivory trail led eastwards, through a tangle of tall mupani trees to a fountain called by the tribespeople *Senkhuwa* from the great wild figtrees (*nkhuwa*), which in former days shed their cool shadows there for man and their wild fruits for the monkeys.

In some odd way a European name became attached to this solitary spot, and today it is still known as Klopperfontein. Hans Klopper, who left his name upon the place, was a slightly built, fair-faced, long-bearded man when Bvekenya met him, living on his farm a few miles south of Louis Trichardt. He had hunted in the area much in former years and Klopperfontein had been his favourite camp.

The fountain was used generally as a short resting place on the ivory trail. The evening stop after Sikokololo's garden was at the rise known as Baobab Hill, where one solitary *shimuwu* (baobab) tree lifted its bloated trunk and tentacle branches to the heavens, like a grim old god of an ancient world summoning his vegetable followers to worship.

Travelling the trail to Baobab Hill generally brought the wanderer a few tales of adventure. Every African wagonboy worthy of his salt had a fund of stories of the trail. It was a trail where the lions slept by the wayside in the heat of the day, where the antelope gambolled in the cool of the night, and where dawn saw man's footprints of the previous day well covered by the tracks of the things of the night: the hyenas, the leopards, the lions and the snakes.

It was a trail along whose length it was easy, and fatal, to drowse. Joseph Fourie, one of the hunters of old, was riding along once to Baobab Hill. He was half asleep in the heat, his horse plodding on with its eyes half closed. From the grass, a leopard suddenly sprang and seized the horse's mouth.

Both rider and horse awoke with a shock. Just what had possessed the leopard to make such a desperate attack remains unknown. He hung on to the horse's mouth like a spotted vampire. The horse wheeled round and round in an agonised effort to shake the fiend off.

Old Joseph was twisted dizzy before he was half awake. He held on to his wits and his horse as stubbornly as the leopard clung to the animal's mouth. When he had recovered from his shock, Joseph reached for his gun, slipped a cartridge in the breech, put the barrel against the leopard's head and blew the devilment out of it. He drowsed no more as he rode to Baobab Hill.

On the western side of Baobab Hill there was water in a trickling streamlet, while on the eastern slope there was an outspan place on a small flat shelf of ground. In after years, Bvekenya was to use this outspan so often that he found it convenient to erect a permanent lion-proof kraal there to shelter his animals.

The kraal was certainly needed at Baobab Hill. Once Bvekenya outspanned there and, with sunset, ordered his servants to put the donkeys into the kraal as usual. He made his bed, dined on a buffalo's tongue, and then wandered out to see the stars before he went to sleep.

To his annoyance, Bvekenya saw seven of his donkeys still roaming about in the shadows. He went up to drive them back into the kraal, but they moved off hastily into the bush. He went back into the kraal to fetch a whip, and irritably turned his servants out of their beds.

"Why don't you do what you're told?" he said, and gave them a kick. "Get the donkeys in before the lions get them."

They went out, rubbing their eyes, protesting, and very puzzled, calling the donkeys and cracking their whips. In a moment they were back in the kraal, piling through the gate so hurriedly that they practically crushed one another to death in the stampede. The donkeys were in all right; but there were seven lions outside, licking their chops in the moonlight.

From Baobab Hill the ivory trail went down to the banks of the Luvuvhu River, to what was known as the drift, or ford, of Makhuleke. At this place, after miles of easy-going, turgid travel, the river suddenly awoke, to go rushing over a shallow, rocky rapid in a flurry of cool movement and sparkling light before relapsing once more into its usual lazy flow.

The ford across the shallows was all shade and reflections. A crowd of wild figtrees stood gathered around the drift, with their roots exposed in a tangled mass by floods long past. Like gnarled old Shangane women, the wild figs lounged on the banks of the river, their roots held out to the rays of the sun, while one or two stood right in the water, as though doing their washing.

Bvekenya rumbled through the ford in his donkey wagon and for the first time found himself on the far bank, in the notorious Crooks Corner. For two and a half miles more his donkeys dragged his wagon, through a mixture of bush and a few Shangane fields, where the cornwives cursed them as they snatched mouthfuls from the maize in passing.

Then came the last laborious heave up the ridge to Makhuleke; and he had reached the end of the road and the final jumping-off ground to adventure.

The store received him in surprise. The crowd of Shangane customers sitting on the veranda stopped their chatter and stared at him in astonished silence. For the first time Bvekenya realised that, if he was finding this new world interesting, then it was equally intrigued by him. He had on a Mexican hat, a red and yellow checked shirt, khaki trousers, and a green bandana slung casually around his neck. A large American police-type revolver, a can opener and a sizable knife dangled from his belt.

He walked up the steps and shouldered his way inside the shop. The atmosphere made his eyes smart. Alec Thompson, serving inside, regarded him without enthusiasm. Bvekenya looked like a dude; and visitors of that type were more nuisance than profit to any storekeeper, respectable or not, in Crooks Corner.

Still, Thompson, a nondescript individual who permanently looked as though he had shaved a week before, made the visitor reasonably welcome. There were three rondavels attached to the store, and in one of them that night Bvekenya told Thompson of his plans.

Many people had told Thompson of similar hopes for fortune on the ivory trail. He had received some quiet amusement from their tales if nothing else, and company was always welcome at that lonely little store. Thompson lighted his one broken oil lamp, produced a store of gin, and was nothing loath to spend the night in yarning: It was a miserable place to be on your own. The days were a curse with the heat, the nights too long to let a man rest in peace. Always he awoke in the early hours and lay listening to the silence, with only the far-off rumble of a lion's roar, or the crack of some elephant pushing a tree over, to mark the passing of the hours.

Some odd characters had certainly found their way to the store at Makhuleke. They came down the trail to hunt elephants, recruit native labour for the mines, or search for Kruger's famous millions. If they gained no profit from their travels, the visitors had nearly all contributed their share to the legends of Crooks Corner. There was that renowned Witwatersrand character, the "Only Jones", the self-styled only member of his numerous clan who ever told the truth. He came down to Crooks Corner searching for diamonds with a party of prospectors. They had no luck.

There was Pat Fay, an old Irish policeman, pensioned off from the police post at Sibasa. He ate so much, he ate all his pension money away and turned gunrunner to raise more cash. Like most of the many others who came to Makhuleke, he had little success. He returned from a long trek once, lean and famished. He sat down to a roasted ox that night and ate himself to death. Many others had reached a similar end through over-nourishment from a bottle; but Pat Fay, in his way, was certainly different. If most of the other shacks scattered about in the bush had a pile of empty bottles outside the back door or window, his hut had just a mound of empty tins on which the roosters perched to crow. They buried him at Elim Mission, a hundred miles away, in a coffin made from canned meat cases; and Makhuleke knew him no more.

All these characters, and many more, had Thompson known. They had come and gone, and left only stories of themselves behind. He told Bvekenya of them, their doings and their hopes, until the lamp went out and the two men slept.

The next day Bvekenya wandered around Crooks Corner, hoping to learn from the experience of its residents. They were a curious crowd. It was difficult to know who was at home and who was not. Their shacks were unsociably scattered in the bush, miles apart. Rumour had it that the men of Crooks Corner liked one another so well that two of them had recently threatened to shoot each other on sight. Some of the huts were deserted, their owners away hunting or adventuring somewhere in the bush; others seemed occupied, although nobody answered the door.

Some of the owners were known to hide in the bush or under the beds if visitors appeared. A few made an appearance, some friendly others surly, and told Bvekenya whatever they knew of the whereabouts of elephants, the prospects of hunting, and the conditions he would encounter in the bush. Most were prepared to talk to him about everything except themselves. Few of them claimed to be hunters; recruiting was an easier way of life.

The most loquacious of all the inhabitants of Crooks Corner was the Irishman William Pye: a short, sandy-haired character, formerly a regular soldier, with a fund of humour, who was always laughing. Pye was a man who had been knocking around in the bush for half his life. In former years he had run the store at the Louis Moore mine. Then he had wandered off to Crooks Corner, built himself a hut, and earned a precarious existence as a recruiter of native labour for the mines and transport rider for the store.

Like his fellow suburbanites, Pye lived largely on quinine and whisky: a diet which had produced an interesting effect on his complexion. Shangane-made marula beer and lala palm wine afforded him some liquid variety, while the few kudu, waterbuck and smaller antelope living in the bush occasionally provided him with something solid if he ever felt hungry.

Pye's residence was a well-known point in Crooks Corner. Adjoining his hut was the local cemetery. In it, so far, eleven adventurers had reached their journey's end as a result of fever, liquor, or the wild animals. Pye was very proud of the place. He always delighted in showing visitors around, telling stories of the occupants, and, like a salesman in real estate, extolling the virtues of certain unoccupied corners in case the visitor had ideas of "settling".

Bvekenya stood the chatter for half an hour and then indicated his fixed desire both to live and to wander. Pye was slightly disappointed.

"A pity," he grumbled. "That's about the best corner left. All you need do is retire for the night with a gallon of Khombo's special brew of marula beer, with a dash of methylated spirits for bitters, and you'd be there by morning. Still, you'll be back. You're young, with lots to learn."

He ushered Bvekenya into his hut. The place was comfortably furnished with empty bottles and a pot of mealie porridge. Pye spent most of his time there. Occasionally he went over and stayed with Thompson in the store, but the two soon grew tired of each other. When tempers became frayed Pye would come home again. His hut was not large. He slept on the floor and reckoned it was cooler there. The conveniences were in the bush and the bathroom consisted of enough space between bottles for one to have a good scratch.

Pye kept female company. One of his latest was standing in the hut when the two men entered. She was as black as night, with a touch of stars in her eyes, blubber lips and legs half as thick as an elephant's. Bvekenya was surprised. He had seen more handsome African women by far.

"You clear out," said Pye, "and cook food."

The girl slipped out. Pye grunted as he saw Bvekenya's face.

"She's all right," he said. "I grant you there's some who look better, but they smell more. The Zulus are real handsome, but most of them make your eyes water."

He surveyed Bvekenya's embarrassment with composure.

"What's the matter? You think this is bad? You think it unusual? Watch out you're not doing the same thing before you know where you are. These things happen in the bush you know; and they don't only happen to Britishers. Let's not have any illusions about that. If half the Dutchmen in Southern Africa had some bloke draw up their family tree they'd mistake the result for a mourning card, for the border would be edged with black.

"The Calvinists and the Roman Catholics put on a smug air, but they still do it. The only difference with them is that they fool themselves they have God on their side, like a crooked referee at a rugby match, and they can get away with all the dirt they like, while it's hell fires for everyone else."

Bvekenya changed the subject hurriedly.

Pye knew little of elephants. He was a recruiter and no hunter. He stayed where he was, did as little as he could, and was happy. His philosophy in life was "to hell with the king, governments and mosquitoes". They were all pests.

"You want elephants?" he asked. "My boy, you want trouble, and you'll get it; and when you've got it, if you can still walk, come back here. Recruiting's easier; and if you want to know why so many of us live here in the bush, I'll tell you. Crooks Corner, they call this. Well, at the corner, where the rivers meet, there's a wonderfully handy beacon. East of it is Portuguese land; north of it is Rhodesia; west of it is this new-fangled Union of South Africa; and south of it is what they want to call a game reserve.

"If you ever get into trouble, just remember that beacon. That's why most of us live here. Whoever comes for you, you can always be on the other side in someone else's territory; and if they all come at once, you can always sit on the beacon top and let them fight over who is to pinch you."

This was the secret of Crooks Corner, which Bvekenya long remembered. It was certainly a convenient beacon. Long afterwards he made a semi-permanent camp at its site and prized the beacon loose. If anybody did come for him he simply moved the beacon, and placed himself in safety without the necessity of breaking camp.

There was little else that Pye could tell him. In any case, the milestones of knowledge along the ivory trail are only learned the hard way, by personal experience; and Bvekenya was to have enough of that.

Two days later, he packed his camp kit and provisions on the backs of his mule and four of his donkeys and set out on his great adventure. He left his wagon and the remainder of his donkeys behind him at the store. Thompson and Pye watched him go without concern. Whether he reached the end of his trail dead or alive worried them not a jot. They had warned him of the dangers which lay ahead, and beyond that could do nothing.

"That's certainly a bloke looking for trouble, instead of running away from it," muttered Thompson, as Bvekenya vanished down the rise.

Pye grunted, and the two men started their morning search for shade.

THREE

A path through the wilds

From the store at Makhuleke a whole complexity of paths radiated off into the blue. Trading paths were tramped along the banks of the river to far-off ports by the sea. There were hunting paths wandering into the bush, with no other purpose than to find the haunts of the game animals; and there were the paths of the game themselves – disjointed, erratic animal highways, wandering from grazing grounds to water-holes, and losing themselves in the secret places of the bush.

Bvekenya followed one of the oldest of all these man-made highways through the bush: the traders' path to Sofala, which swung across the Limpopo and made its way up to the north with many a twist and contortion.

It was a hard year in which Bvekenya commenced his adventures. It was the second season of a drought which had withered even the thornbush, dried the water-holes, and reduced both men and animals to starvation.

Bvekenya walked across the Limpopo in a cloud of dust. The whole course of his journey lay through a land tormented by the devils of heat and thirst. He had half expected to find adventure, elephants and fortune around every bend in that tortuous path, but instead he learned only of the great hunger that comes to the wilds when the rain gods fail to work their magic.

Bvekenya's immediate destination was the Portuguese administrative post of Massangena, 150 miles away on the Great Save River. His purpose was to obtain a hunter's permit, giving him licence to shoot elephants and find a market for their ivory.

Every mile was a long one on the path to Massangena. The Portuguese country in East Africa is a sandy flatness, a vastness seemingly without end, with mupani bush filling up the hollows and river valleys and a variety of wild mahogany, teak and flowering aloes scattered elsewhere.

The narrow pathway had little traffic in times of drought. The life of the country seemed to have dried up along with the rivers and water-holes. No pedlars tramped along the path, for the tribespeople had nothing left to trade. Only a few Shanganes met him on the way, passing along to work on the mines. They told Bvekenya of the remaining water-holes; and the information was invaluable, for there was little left to drink in that parched land, save the product of a few scattered brackish wells sunk by the tribesmen in the beds of former pools.

There was very little game. Occasionally a little Sharpe's grysbok would venture near the path and find its way into his pot, but for most of the journey his gun was silent. He had to supplement supplies by occasionally buying a goat (more than half starved) from the few Shangane kraals he passed on the way.

The hand of the drought was visible on all sides. Every dried up water-hole had the relics of some unfortunate animals around it, who had, perhaps, travelled many a weary mile through the bush to satisfy their thirst, and not possessed the strength or heart to go on elsewhere when they found the old pool vanished.

Hlolwa (the wild dog) was much in evidence among the dead beside these water-holes. Most feared and hated of all the hunters of the wilds, he was the most helpless of all against the drought. He was always the first to die, for even a day without water could mean death to him, and his passing was lamented by none.

The vultures and hyenas, the undertakers of the bush, had profited from the drought in its early stages; but in the end the thirst had caught up with them. If a vulture was left watching in the sky, he was so high and far away that he was beyond the sight of the travellers on the Sofala path. The bush seemed empty even of scavengers. All Bvekenya saw was the corpse of one hyena lying beside the path, with its jaws inextricably caught in the shell of a tortoise, a last mouthful which had proved too much even for the bone-crushing teeth of that over-voracious creature, who had choked himself to death after a wild run through the bush.

It was a dreary journey along the path from one befouled water-hole to another, and Massangena, when he reached it, hardly presented a cheerful picture. The place consisted of a few huts erected on the south bank of the Great Save river. In a normal season a little boat would ferry supplies up the river to the village, but even the Great Save was only a river in name that year. All the water it contained lay in a succession of turgid pools, in which the surviving fish, crocodiles and hippos contended for existence.

Bvekenya, after his fourteen days of dusty travelling, hardly looked an attractive sight himself. Water had never been in sufficient quantity to provide a decent wash. In his final packing he had also neglected to include either razor or scissors, and the absence of these items had its due effect. In short, in his cowboy outfit, with matted hair, a two weeks' growth of beard, and fingernails with most of the dust of Africa beneath them, he looked like a wild man.

There were two Portuguese at the post of Massangena. Bvekenya never learned their real names. The one was known as *Amorina* to the Africans. He was the local administrative head, the *Chef de Post*; a well set up, but flabby man, with the usual yellow complexion produced by the blend of neat brandy and too much quinine. His sole European companion in the post was his secretary, a jumpy little man, wearing trousers too big for him. He was called *Mangone* by the Shanganes.

There were few visitors at Massangena, except unwelcome ones. The place was neither accessible nor desirable, and few people visited it voluntarily. Bvekenya rode into the place with a whoop, on the back of his mule. A few Shanganes put their heads around their doors and stared at him; but there was no other sign of life, apart from one donkey mare, who eyed his mule with disdain and walked away. He dismounted at the office and strode through the door without any sign of an enthusiastic welcome.

The office was furnished with a desk, an out-of-date calendar and the two Portuguese, drinking gin out of one grubby tumbler. Both of them looked as though they would have jumped out of the back window and hidden in the bush if they had known anyone was coming. Amorina was sunk down behind his desk, while Mangone was hiding behind the door. In a back office a Shangane policeman named Folage was questioning an African prisoner by the simple expedient of kicking him in the ribs.

Bvekenya looked at the Portuguese in surprise.

"What's the matter?" he asked, and then repeated the question in Shangane, the only language they were likely to have in common. The Portuguese seemed speechless. Folage stared at him from the other room and spat in some distaste on his prisoner. Bvekenya went to a mirror hanging on one wall and had a look at himself. What he saw made him realise that he would have to do some explaining. He looked like a cross between an ashcan and a pirate.

He told them in stumbling Shangane who he was and what he wanted. They recovered somewhat, and Folage went on kicking his prisoner. It was an occupation in which he seemed to have some skill. Somebody else appeared to have kicked him in times gone by, and his nose had been so well broken by an upward thrust that his nostrils were practically parallel to his face. The result was not handsome.

Amorina recovered enough to shake his head vigorously at the request for a shooting licence. Trying to argue the point in such Shangane as Bvekenya had learned in the past few weeks hardly clarified matters.

Bvekenya produced his money belt after a contorted process of half undressing, which, judging from their expressions, kept the Portuguese in doubt to the last as to whether he was going to produce a gun or start scratching himself.

The sight of his money certainly interested the two men. The sovereigns meant the same in all languages. The Portuguese eyed them with real regret. With a sigh, the Chef de Post scratched around in a drawer and produced an official document whose wording, so far as Bvekenya could make out, seemed to indicate that it was a closed hunting season and there was nothing Bvekenya or the local Portuguese could do. He could shoot for the pot, with limitations, and nothing more.

That was the end of negotiations. He spent the evening with the two administrators, but it was hardly convivial. They drank in company and were bitten by the same mosquitoes. The Portuguese tried to question him about his origin and intentions, but they didn't understand one another sufficiently well to progress in conversation. Bvekenya half-heartedly tried to bribe his way into a licence; but his hosts, with a regret that was touching, declined. What he offered certainly seemed to interest them. They counted his money, asked him what he had in the way of livestock and weapons, and discussed him between themselves with a wealth of detail which he would have loved to understand.

It was not the pleasantest place in which Bvekenya had ever been. He slept uneasily, but nobody disturbed him. The Portuguese were as hospitable as they usually are in such lonely places. With the morning, they breakfasted and then saw him off: Amorina, Mangone and Folage standing on the veranda of their office, watching in silence as he mounted his mule and rode out of the village, towards the west.

Bvekenya went up the Great Save River when he left Massangena. He was in some doubt as to what to do, now that his first plans had miscarried. The idea of moving on into Rhodesia, and perhaps working his way up into Central Africa, seemed the most attractive possibility; but it was useless to consider any really long journey until the weather broke. For the present, the logical thing seemed to be to find some spot where there was a reliable supply of drinking water and pitch a camp until such time as the rains came, making it possible, and convenient, to travel once more.

In this indecisive manner he travelled on up the banks of the Great Save, camping each night by the side of some pool and living on the rietbok and grysbok he found grazing among the reeds.

While loitering around in this fashion, he met another amateur hunter named Fred Roux: a tall, sallow chap, with shifty eyes and dubious intentions, who travelled with him for a while; but they agreed on little save the climate and soon went their respective ways.

Hunting along the banks of the Save was not productive of much profit. Even there, where there was some water, game was scarce; and just how keen the competition was among the hunters Bvekenya was soon to learn.

One morning – hot and breathless – he saw a bushbuck ram moving down a pathway through the reeds to drink. It was a good ram, thin, of course, because of the drought, but big; and the thought of its fine venison spurred Bvekenya on.

He had little trouble in his first shot. There was no wind, and he had hardly to move to bring the ram within range. The shot sent a thousand echoes and splashes down the river. He saw the ram jump, fall, then pick itself up and stumble off into the reeds.

Exulting, he ran forward. It would be a good plan in future, he thought, to build a hide overlooking one of these paths to a water-hole and simply sit and wait for game to come into his bag, instead of laboriously hunting in the heat.

He heard the bushbuck grunting in the reeds. The rams can be dangerous when wounded in such a fine place for an ambush as a clump of reeds. He ran along the game path with great caution. It was always safer to keep a wounded animal in sight, but in thick reeds it was impossible.

The path ran through reeds eight feet high, growing beside a narrow canal ten feet wide and about one mile long, connecting the river proper to a shallow lakelet known as Zambaletshe, which existed on such overflow from the river as the canal could bring it in times of flood. The lakelet was a fine feeding ground for barbel and tiger fish, and the canal was the link through which they swam from river to lake.

If Bvekenya thought of waiting in ambush on the game paths, other and older hunters had long laid their traps in the canal. The splashes Bvekenya had heard when he shot the bushbuck came from the crocodiles. A whole tribe of them lived along that narrow canal by ambushing the fish as they swam through its length.

Bvekenya wasn't used to crocodiles. In fact, he was still an amateur, with much to learn about most game; but as for crocodiles, he had never even seen one close up. The gap in his knowledge was soon filled. The crocodiles had scattered at the sound of his shot, but not all of them had jumped into the river. One old fellow had become slightly confused about what was happening and had also smelled the wounded bushbuck. Running along the path, his eyes fixed ahead trying to spot the bushbuck, Bvekenya saw what he thought to be a tree-trunk lying across the path. He was right on top if it before it came to life with a paralysing jerk.

Each would-be hunter was as surprised as the other. Bvekenya skidded to a stop and tumbled over backwards. He hardly touched the ground before he was up and out of the reeds. A noise like a tornado and a mighty splash told him what had happened to the crocodile. It was not a giant crocodile, but big enough (about twelve feet) to be a nightmare in the reeds, and Bvekenya remembered the meeting long afterwards.

He did not return to the reeds. Fortunately there was no need to resume the hunt. The noise of the surprise encounter had driven the bushbuck out into the open. Bvekenya heard it grunting on the other side of the reeds. He ran around hurriedly and found the animal dying from a bullet through the lungs. He ended its pain with a quick shot – he never found pleasure in the death pangs of an animal – and then dragged it safely out of what he considered to be the reach of the crocodiles.

He still had much to learn of these underwater pirates. On dry land they could raid far, and with horrible effect. Years afterwards he really learned to appreciate the daring of a crocodile on land. On the lower Save he once saw a young lion kill a waterbuck about a hundred yards from the river. Bvekenya was hunting elephant at the time and was loath to disturb his quarry by firing at the lion or otherwise disturbing the normal course of events.

Accordingly, he hid behind the trees and was the silent witness of a curious battle. Two big black crocodiles, strong and impudent, clambered out of the river. They made straight for the astonished lion. The bigger crocodile, an old male who, from his attitude, didn't give a damn for anything or anybody, made no bones about his mood. Snapping a pair of jaws, like a surgeon sharpening a trepan over a prostrate patient, he headed straight for the lion.

The lion stood his ground for perhaps something longer than a second, but not much more. He turned tail and ran for the bush. The second crocodile, meanwhile, had seized the carcass of the waterbuck and dragged it backwards into the water. The retreating lion glimpsed its vanishing dinner out of the corner of its eye. The animal made a half-hearted effort to get back to the river; but the big, aggressive crocodile would have none of it. The more pugnacious of the two raiders planted itself squarely between the dismayed lion and the crocodile dragging the carcass off and offered to do battle. All the lion had the nerve to do was growl his chagrin and rage at the two crocodiles disappearing back into the river with their booty. The lion was left sitting crestfallen on the banks. Bvekenya kept his peace and marvelled.

One lesson Bvekenya did learn from the encounter with his first crocodile was to keep his camps a prudent distance from rivers. He made what he intended to be his permanent camp until the drought broke on a small hillock overlooking the junction of the Pembe and the Save rivers. It was a fine site for a camp, with a tall leafy tree casting its shade, and the slight elevation of the hillock providing a commanding view across the bush.

At this place, Bvekenya made himself comfortable and prepared for a long stay. The camp had everything he could have desired, considering the poverty of the country; and yet, curiously, he never felt at ease there. Some foreboding of trouble seemed to worry him with the persistence of a subdued toothache. He could not understand it. He was too inexperienced in the wilderness to realise the implications of his feeling. He tried to dismiss it as simply a foolish whim. His camp was safe, snug and sheltered. The few scraggy

Shanganes in the area were too famished to do anything other than search for roots and berries. There seemed to be no possible source of danger, and still he was uneasy, no matter how hard he tried to banish the feeling from his mind.

He had many distractions to occupy his thoughts at this camp. The struggle to remain alive kept him busy all through the hot days. Hunting occupied his time. If he had venison, then he could exchange his surplus with the tribespeople for the wild berries their women found in the bush and the fish they caught with their traps in the river pools.

There was more game around his new camp than he had so far seen anywhere else, for the water in the deep river pools attracted animals from a vast surrounding area of drought-stricken bush.

But it was not only game that was attracted to the pools. Every predatory hunter for miles around seemed to have followed the antelope to the water, and found a new lair for himself in the tangled undergrowth and overhanging cliffs along the banks of the river.

Life was not only strenuous but also dangerous, and competition among the hunters was keen. Bvekenya was cautious, but otherwise he did not mind the lions or the leopards: they were the legitimate hunters of the wilderness. They competed with him for the game, but despite the great hunger that comes with drought they had not turned man-eater; and at night, sitting in the solitude of his camp, he found a strange sense of companionship in the distant rumble of a lion's roar, or the more sinister coughing of a leopard. He would wonder what they had killed out there in the shadows. When the leopards raided the troops of baboons sleeping in the river trees he would listen with amusement to the wild outburst of cursing and screaming from the old dog baboons – and when the dawn came he would watch with interest as the scattered members of the monkey troops endeavoured to extricate themselves from the furthest tips of the thorn trees, where their terror had driven them to find a precarious and oft-times painful refuge.

All these things kept Bvekenya preoccupied and gave his eager mind much to observe and learn of the way of the wilds; and yet the ever-present sense of foreboding never left him. There seemed to be something in the air, as oppressive as an approaching thunderstorm.

That inarticulate and mysterious sixth sense was trying to warn him of something, nudging and tugging at his mind, almost like a faithful dog trying to draw a blind man away from disaster.

As yet, however, he was too inexperienced to realise the full meaning of this incomprehensible mood. It pulled and jostled at his thoughts day and night. In the end he tried with deliberate daydreams to drive the uneasiness away, and it seemed to pass. He was yet to learn that, if one closes one's mind stubbornly to its message, this strange sense withdraws crestfallen; and only long afterwards, from the darkness of the secret shadows of the mind, when one is bitterly lamenting some cruel misfortune, there sometimes comes an echo of: "I told you so, but you paid no heed."

So he came to what was to be his last night at his camp at the junction of the rivers. For thirty nights he had slept in peace at this camp on the hillock, and this last night started with a feeling of contentment which quite smothered the old uneasiness.

He had hunted well that day. An impala doe was lying ready to be cut into biltong, which would keep him for a week. Then, late in the afternoon, he had found a covey of fine, fat, crested guineafowls. As he rummaged through the dead grass along the banks of the river he had heard their peculiar, dry, staccato cry. He had crept upon them with extreme care. Of all dishes in Africa, a crested guineafowl was not to be excelled for flavour.

He had hoped for more, but got one. A go-away bird,

unseen in a tree, had suddenly betrayed him. The birds rose in a sudden flurry of alarm. He just had time to lift his gun and fire. He only had his one Lee Metford .303, but it was a clean hit. The bird exploded in mid-air, like a feather pillow breaking over a schoolboy's head.

Bvekenya ran and picked up the corpse. The bird was still warm and kicking. He stood and looked at it for a minute. In his hand he saw not a feathered bird, but a neatly trussed dinner, with golden drumsticks, rich gravy, and delicious stuffing made from wild herbs. It was what the dictionaries call apperception.

Two hours later, apperception had become reality, and then just a reflective sigh. In the darkness Bvekenya lay in his camp beside his fire, listening to the voice of the wilds and reflecting contentedly on his meal that night. What an end for a bird, he thought lazily. What a culmination to all life's worries and complexities, to give someone else such real delight.

He fell to wondering idly whether any missionary had ever given as much real contentment to his cannibals. The gravy had been truly superb. He lay on his back and lazed luxuriously. Up on its little hillock, the camp was cooler than the plains, where everything was hemmed in by bush. An evening breeze came from the far-off Indian Ocean and stole slyly down his shirt, like a lover fondling his mistress.

Bvekenya worked his shoulders lazily into his grass couch, grinned at the stars, and dozed. What was there to worry about? He could not see the figures stealing through the bush upon him. He was delightfully tired. He fell asleep. It was a calm night, full of dreams.

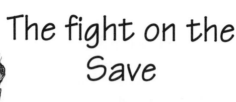

FOUR

The fight on the Save

When that first strange wave of restlessness passes through the sleeping world at the false dawn, like the advance murmur of a new breeze rustling the leaves into wakefulness, and the creatures of the wilds all greet this sign of a new day with their calls, catastrophe came to Bvekenya.

A crowd of Shanganes, creeping up silently through the bush, suddenly took his camp with a rush. He was fast asleep, snug and seemingly secure, when the attack came. They jumped the surrounding wall of thornbush and tore inside with a yell.

Bvekenya awoke to the crack of a knobkerrie on his skull. Fortunately, in the dark, it was a glancing blow; but strong enough to teach him that the raiders were hardly there for fun.

Bvekenya reached for his gun. Somebody already had hold of the barrel, for they had seen the metal glinting in the light of the embers of the fire. Bvekenya caught hold of the butt, and at least one of the raiders rued ever taking part in the attack. Bvekenya tried to wrench the gun free. When he found it too securely held, he twisted it around with all his force and pulled the trigger. There was a scream of pain as somebody received a bullet through his leg.

The gun came free. Bvekenya exultantly lifted it up. Before he could reload, a pair of hands like a vice gripped his neck from behind and threw him sideways. He landed on the ground with a thud that almost broke his back. His attacker came down with him, clinging to his throat and locking his arms in by the simple expedient of wrapping his legs around Bvekenya's body.

The gun went flying into the shadows. Bvekenya fought for his life. The stranger seemed glued to him like a horrible, malignant growth. Bvekenya threw himself around with all his strength, but the strangler was a dead weight. His hands seemed as strong as the claws of a lion and his nails were digging into Bvekenya's neck with killing pressure.

Bvekenya twisted on his stomach, with the strangler on his back. He had little strength left. His head was booming and throbbing. His eyes were dilated, and vision was just a crazy display of spots and flashes.

All he could see were the embers of the fire beside which he had been sleeping. They gave him a last hope. With his remaining strength, he arched his back and kicked himself over like a bucking bronco. The strangler toppled with him, sideways into the embers.

There was a howl of agony from the man, and the claw-like hands came free. Bvekenya gulped a mixture of fresh air, smoke, and the smell of his own clothes and flesh burning. He rolled off the embers and staggered to his feet.

The strangler pounced at him across the fire. Bvekenya met him, still on his knees. The strangler tried to get his hands around Bvekenya's neck again. This time things were different, Bvekenya was facing his attacker; but whatever he did he had to do fast. The strangler was menace enough, but milling around were the rest of the raiders, only desisting from attack for fear of hitting their own comrade.

As the strangler's hands groped for his neck, Bvekenya lunged upwards. He found the man's face and felt for the nostrils, intending to force them back. They seemed to be curiously placed. Through his mind flashed a picture of the hideous Folage. The nostrils were certainly the same, broken and forced back in some past encounter.

Bvekenya had no more time for identification. The man, whoever he was, had no nose; but he had eyes. Bvekenya found the left eye with his thumb, and his nail dug at it. He felt the strangler stiffen, but the hands still clawed at his throat. He dug his thumb into the eye with fury. For a moment it held. Then Bvekenya felt it break in a horrible mess of blood and skin, like forcing his thumb into an orange.

The strangler went mad with pain. He screamed, with a ghastly mixture of agony and terror. Bvekenya scrambled to his feet. He ducked between two shadowy figures and, without hesitation, jumped the wall of thorn bush. He half rolled, half scrambled, down the hillock, every moment fearing that someone would jump down on him. He reached the banks of the Save and went straight on into the water without thought of crocodiles. If there were any of those brutes present, they had already been alarmed by the clamour in the camp. With fear to speed him across, Bvekenya swam the river, scrambled up the opposite bank and raced off through the reeds to safety.

No attempt was made to pursue him across the river. Some of the raiders chased him down the hillock to the water's edge, but there they stopped. They threw a few clubs at his head as he swam, but without scoring a hit. Then they turned and went back to the camp. From the other side of the river, he had the mortification of hearing (rather than seeing them in the dim light) as they looted his belongings. The would-be strangler was still moaning as his companions attended him, but the rest of the attackers busied themselves in rounding up Bvekenya's donkeys and mule, counting his money, squabbling among themselves over possession of his rifles and ammunition, and scrambling for his food and other trifles. With several hangers-on, who joined the raiders after the attack, the gang seemed about twenty strong.

Bvekenya was in a sad way. He was practically naked, with not a possession left save for the pair of cotton underpants in which he had gone to sleep. He hardly knew what to do. Around him lay the wilderness, its only friendly thing the pathway leading back to Makhuleke, some 150 miles away.

It was useless to stay where he was. At any moment the raiders could decide to track him down. The path had been wearisome enough when he had food, draught animals and a gun. What it would be like when he had nothing, he could scarcely imagine; and yet what was he to do? Very down-hearted, he started to trudge back to Makhuleke.

The sun came up and looked down upon him with hostility. His nakedness seemed to be an offence to the wilderness. The thorns tore at him, and the sun scorched down upon his head and back.

He tramped along to the junction of the Save and the Lundi rivers before the heat became too much for him. He found some shade and passed the hot hours in plaiting a hat from lala palm leaves.

Later that afternoon he started off again. Towards evening he met a party of Shanganes, returning home from working on the mines. They regarded him in blank astonishment. To encounter a white man at all along that path would have been an event; to encounter a white man in Bvekenya's condition was something incredible.

Bvekenya told them of his misfortune. They listened to him in wonder, with many a click of sympathy. At the end of the tale their leader, Matlharene, was as kindly as he could be. The Shanganes had very little they could give Bvekenya. They had been driven out of their homes to work by the drought. They had worked the shortest contract period possible and were hastening home with what little money they had earned, hoping that the families they had left behind were still alive.

The Shanganes, however, gave Bvekenya the haunch of a goat they had acquired. They contributed a few scraps of clothing and gave him much practical advice as to the best route to follow home: the path running directly along the Rhodesian border, where there was more water and where the resident tribespeople were more friendly than elsewhere.

With a final present of a spear, with which to defend himself, and an old knapsack, to clean and sew up with sinews as a water container, they saw him on his way and watched him trudge off along the pathway to the Limpopo with genuine sympathy. They were the first to name him *Bvekenya*, for as he went on the hot sand burned his feet and made him appear to swagger as he walked.

The 150-mile walk was a nightmare. He walked at night mostly, when it was cooler, and slept in the shade during the heat of the day. Even this precaution did not quite save him from the sun. Not even the elephants are immune from sunstroke in the African wilderness. Fever also came, although the mosquitoes were not bad in that time of drought.

Nevertheless, many days of his journey became blanks in his memory. Just how long it took to tramp the 150 miles he never knew. When he felt a bout of fever or sunstroke approaching, he sought shelter beneath some tree and left the spear in the ground pointing in the direction he wanted to go, so that he would not turn back in mistake while he was half off his head in delirium.

Fortunately, he encountered few wild animals. One or two hyenas saw him on the path and followed him for a few miles hoping he was going to die; but he had no serious trouble. The game was all concentrated on the banks of the few rivers which still contained water, and the lions and leopards were off hunting there.

Water-holes were few and very far between. He would walk for hours, with his thirst mounting to an intolerable craving, chewing on leaves in an effort to find relief. Always he found water at the end of the stage; but the stages were long and the water generally just a dirty, semi-solid fluid when he reached it.

Before half of the journey was over his whole body was wizened and dry. He had shrunk appreciably, but felt as though his skin was still too small for him.

At some of the holes, where there was sufficient water, he slept up to his neck in the mud and liquid filth; but it was a luxury to find places where he could do this. When he did ease his body into these mud-holes his very skin seemed to absorb water like blotting paper, and for a few hours he would find a relief that was heavenly. He learned then just what real pleasure an animal must find in wallowing in the mud. These mud-holes, and the occasional Shangane kraals at places such as Slotele, were the only relief on his whole journey and the only comfort, even though it consisted simply of mud from the holes, and maybe a handful of dried wild oranges from some poverty-stricken but kindly tribesman.

Like the elephants and the buffaloes, he found it a convenience to keep his skin covered in mud. The mud not only protected him from the sun, but it also gave him some defence against the swarms of insects which attacked him. After all the years of drought in the bush, the insects were as thirsty as whole armies of troopers. They would attack like a plague anything which seemed to contain moisture, sucking and biting at any animal, trying to get a drink, until they drove the creature half insane. Only mud was a defence, and the thicker the better.

At one place, Pangale, Bvekenya slept under a baobab tree. He awoke to a terrific humming noise. The whole air seemed to be alive with insects, especially bees, who were sucking water out of his little knapsack. It was practically a battle to death to drive the swarms off and retrieve the bag, sadly depleted of its precious contents. After that, he plaited dead grass around the knapsack for protection.

He did have one odd experience. One morning, after his usual walk through the night, the path led him to a small water-hole, half lost in the depths of a mupani forest. This was to be the end of his night's walk, where he would rest until evening came again; and he anticipated sleep and water with a keenness only understandable if your whole body is parched and your feet a hideous ache of cuts and tears from thorns and endless miles of sand.

As he approached the water-hole, Bvekenya heard a strange commotion. He stood and listened in surprise for some while. It was obviously the shrill noise of an elephant trumpeting, against a background of dull thuds: like some-body beating a carpet with vigour, and screaming in the process.

Bvekenya went on to the water-hole with caution. What he saw bewildered him. There was an enormous elephant, the first he had so far seen, trumpeting and stamping about around the water, for all the world as though it were a woman holding her skirts up and jumping away from a mouse.

Bvekenya watched the animal in amazement. He carefully worked his way nearer the waterhole, full of curiosity as to the reason for this strange performance. He had half made up his mind that the elephant had gone berserk, when he at last secured a complete view of the proceedings.

On the ground, offering the elephant battle, was *Shid-zidzi*, the tough, little honey-badger, spluttering and cursing with rage in his harsh, spitting voice. The elephant towered eleven feet above Shidzidzi, but he was in a state of complete dismay. The honey-badger was nipping the elephant's feet, and then slipping away as expertly as a boxer when the blundering giant tried to trample him down.

Bvekenya stood watching this strange struggle with fascination. Without thinking, he stepped out of the bush to secure a better view. The elephant saw him immediately. With a dismayed squeal at the appearance of some fresh trouble, the elephant turned tail and fled.

Shidzidzi was completely triumphant. He had not seen Bvekenya. He thought the elephant was running away from him. He practically stood up on his hind legs and shook his fist in defiance. The opportunity was too good for Shidzidzi to miss. To have a whole elephant run away from him was a wonderful achievement. With a chortle of glee, he hurtled off through the bush in pursuit of his fleeing enemy.

Bvekenya walked down to the pool. All around the water the ground was trampled as flat as a tennis court. The battle must have been going on for some time. The only explanation he could think of for so unequal a combat was that this was the honey-badger's private drinking pool, and he objected to the elephant churning it into a wallow. There was a second pool a few hundred feet away. Bvekenya prudently made his resting place there, in case the pugnacious little animal should return, flushed with victory, and start on him.

The eventual sight of the store at Makhuleke was like a glimpse of heaven to a doubting pilgrim. It must have been about twelve days after he started his walk when he reached Crooks Corner, but how much time he had lost through fever and sunstroke he never knew.

The redoubtable Pye was away transport riding when Bvekenya arrived. Thompson received him at the store with more "I told you so's" than anything else; but he was not lacking in sympathy. Bvekenya washed the mud off his person, had a good meal, and slept for a day.

When he had recovered somewhat, he discussed his misfortune with Thompson. The only thing which really seemed to surprise the trader was the story of the honey-badger and the elephant. Thompson stared at Bvekenya blankly when he heard this.

"Fellow," he said, "you must have had fever bad, to see that; and believe me, you must have fever worse if you're thinking of going back."

Bvekenya discussed his projects with the man in detail, but he received no support for the hopes of vengeance which he nursed.

"All you'll get is another thrashing, and lucky if you get away alive," said Thompson. "I'm telling you, Barnard, they don't like foreigners on the Portuguese side. In any case, the place is run by the police boys; they do just about what they like, and most of them are bigger thieves than the criminals. You'll have everything against you if you go back. The bush is tough enough, without fighting a one-man war in it against Portugal, the natives and the elephants."

Bvekenya had the stubbornness of youth. He had thought the matter over all through his long walk back. At times, the hope of vengeance was about the only thing to sustain him. He felt that if he simply abandoned his hopes and left the bush behind him he would consider himself a coward for the rest of his life. The beating rankled in his mind. For long hours on the path, when his feet ached and he was almost off his head for want of water, he had raged at the Portuguese at Massangena and at the raiders who had caught him so easily when he was fast asleep.

Thompson shrugged his shoulders at Bvekenya's decision to return.

"What do you want me to do?" he asked.

Bvekenya's most pressing need was for money. Here Thompson could help him. The trader advanced £45 against the security of Bvekenya's wagon, and gave him some old garments to act as temporary clothes. With this money, and slightly better clad, Bvekenya set off back along the ivory trail, with Johannesburg as his destination. His intention was to gather his remaining savings, invest in a new rifle and equipment, and then stake his all on a return to the bush.

The journey back to civilisation was miserable, and the miles could not pass fast enough for him. Every resident of Crooks Corner, and all the traders he met along the way, were of one opinion in advising him not to return; and their forebodings certainly did not make things easier for him.

He reached Monty Ash's store at Papazela, near Klein Letaba; and that fever-stricken but kind-hearted man added the weight of his lifetime of experience in the bush to the advice of all those who had told Bvekenya to go home.

The young man was certainly disturbed by the solid front of opinion against his project of vengeance, but still he persisted. He left his two donkeys in the care of Monty Ash and begged a lift on a wagon as far as Soekmekaar.

The railway from Pietersburg to the north was then in the throes of construction. At the railhead there was a store, doing a roaring business and run by a shifty-eyed little Jew, whose principal recreation seemed to be to read his prayer books aloud in a cracked voice, while candles burned around him in polished brass holders.

Bvekenya disturbed this worthy from his prayers as soon as the wagon dropped him at the railhead. It was early evening, and he was told that a construction ballast train would be leaving within minutes for Pietersburg.

The storeman sold clothing, and he left his religious pre-occupation long enough to sell Bvekenya one of his stock suits, a pair of shoes, underwear and some toilet articles.

With the parcel under his arm, the young man ran out of the shop and scrambled aboard the train as it started to move.

At least his moves for the next few hours were now decided and he could relax. He made his way to the toilet, and for half an hour enjoyed himself as much as one can while having a bath in a basin and shaving off a month's growth of beard with cold water in a swaying railway coach.

At the end, he felt a certain amount of satisfaction. At least civilisation had its advantages, with its conveniences and comforts. He put on his new underwear and nice clean shirt.

Thankfully, he threw his dingy old clothing out of the window for the railway workers to find. Then he opened the parcel containing the suit. It was quite a blow. The trader had not been content with simply overcharging him. The suit was minus the trousers.

He looked out of the window longingly, but his old trousers were miles behind. It was little use cursing. Fortunately he had acquired an old raincoat. He put this on, to hide his shortage of clothing in a lower sphere, and went back fuming to his seat. If anything was calculated by fate to disillusion him about the joys of civilisation, it was this small-scale bit of robbery. He seethed with rage for hours, imagining the little trader reading his books in a sanctimonious voice and chuckling in between paragraphs at having literally stolen the pants off a customer.

At Pietersburg, Bvekenya changed to the normal overnight train to Pretoria. It was hours before the rhythmical beat of the wheels on the rails lulled him to sleep; and then he dreamed strange dreams of Folage, with his broken nose and one of his eyes hanging out, and the wizened little trader, laughing at him across the counter as he counted his money. Both the wilderness and civilisation had, it seemed, their peculiar dangers.

FIVE

The last chance

Bvekenya's visit to Johannesburg was neither lengthy nor pleasant. He changed trains at Pretoria, while its citizens were still rubbing the sleep from their early morning eyes. Johannesburg was just stirring with its first after-breakfast bustle when he arrived at the station, and, among that rush of sophisticated people, found himself a horribly self-conscious character with the wind gleefully intent on blowing his mackintosh around his legs.

He certainly looked a real rustic. His long hair, his old mackintosh and his awkwardness seemed apparent to every member of the passing throng. One group of street urchins attached themselves to his wake and almost giggled him into headlong flight down Eloff Street.

His first objective was a pair of trousers. He was too shy to tell the shopkeeper that he was without a pair. He bought the first trousers offered him, tucked the parcel under his arm, dodged his way back through the crowds in Eloff Street, and returned to the station.

The urchins were still loitering around and watched his search for the toilet rooms with interest. When he was forced to ask one of them for directions, they gleefully led him to the ladies' room and bustled him inside, to the consternation of its occupants.

Eventually he pulled his trousers on, and the feeling of

relief restored his confidence. When he left he could walk as a man again, and the urchins scattered.

A visit to a barber's shop completed his immediate personal needs. Then he busied himself in turning his savings into ready money. Any lingering doubts he may have had on the train about a return to the wilderness had been effectively dispelled by his reception in civilisation. The wilderness had certainly played him a scurvy trick, but at least he had felt at home there. His experiences with the trousers had embarrassed him horribly, and had emphasised his isolation in the midst of the sprawling city. After that, his only desire was to get out of the place as soon as possible.

His short experience in the bush had taught him several valuable lessons. If he was to live in the bush, then he was to live with his gun as his only certain friend. It was necessary, therefore, that he secure a good one. He invested every penny he could spare in a vicious, short-barrelled, 9.5 Mannlicher-Schönauer, with 500 cartridges. With it in his hands, plus a revolver for emergencies, he was confident he could stop all Portugal, let alone a parcel of bush Shanganes and a few crooked policemen.

The question of clothing had also given him food for thought. The ridiculous costume he had affected when he first took the ivory trail made him blush every time he thought of it. What he needed was obviously something less decorative but completely practical.

He spent some hours in the Johannesburg clothing stores, examining every type of garment. In the end he decided on a material which was to remain his life-long favourite and special costume for the bush: Thenceforth he wore greenish-coloured corduroy shorts and a jacket or jersey. The corduroy was superior to plain khaki, for it was absolutely noiseless. Every surplus portion of his clothing was eliminated. Even the pockets were cut off, so that there was nothing which could possibly catch in the bush, either as a warning of his approach or as a hindrance if he fled.

Rubber-soled boots were also selected for their silence, while puttees took precedence over any other type of leggings for the same reason. A big, shady hat, with its sides tucked in so that it did not interfere with his hearing or catch in the thorns, completed his costume. With these items, and a few minor accessories and comforts, he returned to the railway station; and that night, from his compartment window, watched with relief as the lights of the city vanished into the distance, until they seemed but a continuation of the milky-way. If he never saw them again he would be happy. Ahead lay the blackness of the wilderness. He was going to take his last chance there, that he knew. He was certain of one thing only: come what may, if his own future was black, then the future of those who had attacked him was blacker.

The journey back to Crooks Corner was uneventful. On the way he called on the little trader who had done him out of the trousers; but, perhaps fortunately, that worthy was away.

Monty Ash, at Klein Letaba, had kept the two donkeys safely for him. He obviously thought Bvekenya mad ever to have returned, and he made no secret of his opinion. Still, he was a friendly man: very shy of European women but a kindly host to every adventurer who tramped the ivory trail past his door. His advice was always well meant, and his knowledge valuable.

As a parting gift to Bvekenya, Monty gave him an old .303 to use as a trap gun, and then saw him off with regret. Alec Thompson, at Makhuleke, hardly believed it when he recognised Bvekenya again. That anybody could look for trouble so persistently astounded the trader. Bvekenya spent only one night at the store and then, with dawn the next morning, he set off back along that long pathway which had brought him such grief and weariness so short a while before.

If anything, there seemed to be less game on the path than when he had first journeyed along it. By the time he reached the Save he had consumed nearly all the food he had brought with him and had shot nothing. His first concern, therefore, was to replenish his supplies and put his new gun to use.

Bvekenya camped on the Save, but this time on the Rhodesian side of the border, as a precaution against any attack by his old acquaintances. In the remaining pools of the Save there were many hippos, concentrated by the drought; and they provided the best possible chance of securing meat in quantity.

He secreted his camp equipment and store of cartridges in a hollow tree at his camp site and then set out after the hippos. He had no great difficulty in tracking down a suitable target. In a pool at the junction of the Save and Lundi rivers he found a fine big bull hippo, lazing about in the shallows.

Bvekenya disturbed the hippo's daydreams with a bullet that made him sink like a block of concrete. There was hardly even a splash. It was Bvekenya's first really big kill, and the echoes the Mannlicher-Schönauer raised were like a shout of triumph.

He had learned a few of the peculiarities of hippos from the Shanganes. He had selected his shot carefully, remembering their advice: behind the eyes if the animal is sideways, between the eyes if it is a frontal shot. If the hippo splashes after the shot, then he is wounded and most likely will not die. If he sinks in silence, then the shot could not have been better.

No ripple disturbed the pool. Only far off, down the river, a group of hadedah birds sent their strident cry of alarm echoing back, as they sped off between the wooded riverbanks.

It was midday, and he could normally expect the dead hippo to float in three hours. He whiled the time away with a cat-nap in the shade of a tree. It was a long three hours, and even then the hippo showed no signs of floating. Experience was to teach Bvekenya that both the temperature of the water and, more especially, the contents of the animal's stomach, determined the period of time that would elapse before it floated. A full stomach of grass and reeds would bring the carcass to the surface quickly by producing inflationary gases. Conversely, an empty stomach would leave the carcass below water for a much longer period.

Towards evening Bvekenya tired of his long wait and went back to camp. He received a sad shock. While he had dozed a grass fire had swept through the place, and everything he had, if not destroyed, was at least badly scorched. He retrieved what he could; but his blankets were gone, his packsaddles destroyed, and his precious store of mealies so badly scorched that most of them were only fit to be ground up on a stone and turned into a sort of coffee.

He spent a restless night, half sleeping and half cursing the fates for his new misfortune. With the dawn, he went back to the pool and at least had the gratification of seeing the hippo floating on the surface. It was an old, amber-coloured bull, with that reddish tinge to its skin which hippos seem to get as they grow older.

A crowd of Shanganes had already gathered on the banks, like vultures attracted from miles around by a kill. When Bvekenya gave them the signal they swam out gleefully and pushed the carcass to the shore. There was great feasting that day. Bvekenya took the tasty meat from behind the shoulder as his special portion, cut sjamboks from the skin, collected the fat, and made some biltong; but the rest of the carcass was given to the Shanganes, and they made short work of it.

The sight of the famished tribespeople feasting on the hippo, and their gratitude, reminded Bvekenya that he owed a favour to the returning mineworkers who had helped him in his time of trouble. Their kindness had almost certainly saved his life, and it was a debt which he was resolved to repay with interest.

The returning mine labourers had come from the kraal of a petty headman named Shubela, who lived about two days' walk north of the Great Save River, on the path to Sofala. A visit to this kraal was doubly attractive, for an isolated thundercloud had recently passed that way and left behind a belt of green grass and rejuvenated bush: the unmistakable trail of a wandering rain god.

The antelope had flocked to this narrow and temporary belt of greenness and the prospects for hunting were good. Bvekenya, therefore, set off cheerfully on foot to visit his former benefactors, leaving his donkeys on the Lundi, where they were safe from the insidious tsetse fly.

It was a walk made at least slightly more pleasant than usual by the recent rain, and he easily found the kraal. It was a poor sort of place, just about six huts built in a shallow valley full of mupani trees. The place was practically deserted when he reached it. Shubela, a tall, dark Shangane with a long beard, came out to meet him; but he was so thin he could hardly walk. He looked as though he needed a cup of black coffee before he could throw a shadow.

The kraal people were in the last stages of starvation. Every animal the people had ever possessed had died, except one miserable brown dog: a creature so thin that the wind seemed to whistle through its ribs. All the able-bodied males of the place, including the mine labourers, had gone off to Rhodesia in the hope of buying food. Only those of their women and families who still lived were left.

Bvekenya was appalled at the condition of the place. He went off immediately in search of game, and within hours had shot an eland and a hartebeest in the green belt. Old Shubela almost cried when he saw these animals fall. With one other Shangane, who had accompanied Bvekenya from the hippo pool, he helped to cut up the animals. Then they prepared big fires and boiled a rich venison broth. To have given the people meat to eat in their present condition would have been fatal. Instead, Bvekenya doled out rations of broth for three days and the people flourished amazingly. On the fourth day they had their first meat; and the speed with which they recovered their vigour and condition was as astonishing to Bvekenya as had been their original wretched condition.

The kraal's one dog was a particularly remarkable example of rejuvenation. He had certainly never been well fed (fortunate indeed is the kraal dog who is ever better than half-starved) and how he had survived at all was a mystery. Bvekenya used to laugh at him as he fed. He was so weak that he had to keep his legs spread-eagled to hold himself up, and a slight gust of wind would always blow him over. A dozen times and more Bvekenya had to pick the animal up and set him on his feet.

The dog was the kraal's last possession. One evening, when Bvekenya returned from a hunt, the people came to him in a body and presented the animal to him as some slight sign of their gratitude. He accepted the scraggy gift with pleasure – actually he needed a dog for hunting but insisted on presenting the dog's late owner with a limbo (or four feet length) of calico, which was among the very few things that had survived the fire. He named the dog Limbo, from the circumstances of its acquisition, although for the present all it could do was eat.

Every day Bvekenya hunted through the surrounding bush for game. The kraal people possessed no firearms, but in the extremity of their hunger they had sought to trap the game with an intricate variety of snares and pitfalls.

These traps made every pathway a menace. The people warned him of them, but even then he had some narrow shaves. He was walking along a game path once, with his 9.5 on his shoulder and the .303 under his arm, when he barged straight into a cunningly hidden elephant trap.

The first thing he knew of the trap was when the blade of a heavily weighted spear came down with a thud, slipping along his back, tearing his shirt and cracking the butt of his .303. There was consternation among the kraal people when they heard of this. The blades of the trap spears were always poisoned.

From the seeds of the creeper known as *butsulu*, the Shanganes pounded a poisonous powder. They mixed this with wild gum and coated the points of the trap spears. Death came certainly, and painfully, to whatever the spears touched.

Bvekenya could not see whether his back was scratched. There was a numbness where the spear had struck him, but whether this came from a wound, or just from the glancing blow of the shaft, he could not see. He returned to the kraal in some trepidation, determined to shoot himself if he was found to be wounded. Waiting for death from some lingering poison was not his way of losing his life.

While the women wailed and the children set up a great howl, one old woman, the local witch, came and examined him. Fortunately there was no damage beyond a severe bruising. The spear point must have missed him by a fraction of an inch. The relief the old woman's report gave him was the greatest emotional experience he had ever known. He sat half stunned, while the Shanganes laughed around him and the old witch carefully rubbed ointment into his bruises. Within a few days he was better.

He could not remain as the benefactor of the village forever. He stayed with the people, sleeping in a rough camp adjoining the village, until their menfolk returned from Rhodesia. They came trooping back about fourteen days later, with a few miserable loads of foodstuffs on their heads.

The sight of Bvekenya and the news of the relief he had brought to the kraal was almost unbelievable to them. Whatever else Bvekenya had done in his life, this one act certainly made him some firm friends, for the people of that lonely little village in the bush were destined to remember him with gratitude and be his faithful allies all his life.

For another week Bvekenya hunted for the kraal. He taught the people how to make biltong, and with them improvised a technique for preserving meat by boiling it in clay pots until all moisture evaporated and a layer of fat formed over the top as a natural seal and preservative.

He discussed his project of elephant hunting many times with the kraal people. They told him all they knew of the whereabouts of the elephants. Much of their advice was exceedingly practical. The problem of the tsetse fly, for instance, had given him much thought. If he was to shoot elephants, then donkeys to carry the tusks were almost imperative. The difficulty of keeping them alive in fly country was a matter of some urgency.

In African fashion, the Shanganes had long ago devised what they considered to be a specific preventive of the disease. They pointed to Limbo as proof of their medicine. Dogs were as susceptible to the tsetse as anything else, but it had taken a drought to kill off all their animals. Their specific was the practice of feeding a few dead tsetse flies to all their animals. According to their reasoning, this custom (followed by some tribes even with snakes, as an antidote to snake bites) made animals impervious to the fly, if only through digestive familiarity.

Bvekenya was slightly doubtful. He never tried the Shangane specific, but he never lost a donkey to the tsetse in fifteen years. He devised a witch's brew of his own – a mixture of animal fat, Cooper's dip, tree gum and honey – which he smeared over his donkeys. All the flies who landed on the animals stuck fast to the gum, and were poisoned by the arsenic. The donkeys certainly became pretty sticky – walking fly traps in fact – and the specific sounded some-what odd; but at least his animals lived, and that to him seemed proof enough of the mixture's efficiency.

As for elephants, the kraal people were keenly interested in his plans and hopes. They had little doubt of his success. In this the old witch acted as their spokeswoman. She made quite an occasion of her optimism. One evening, while they were sitting around the kraal fire – a cheerful, lively blaze, surrounded by black faces gathered to hear Bvekenya yarning with the men – the old witch came with her bones. Then she threw the bones for Bvekenya, while the kraal people listened intently.

"White man," she said, "you who are our friend and chief. Be not afraid. Truly it was you who saved us from the famine. Are not our ancestors grateful? Did not the spirits save you from the trap?"

The kraal people sounded their assent, from the deep voice of the headman down to the youngest child who could speak.

"You must be careful in the forest," went on the witch. "Tread gently on the paths, leave not your trail for others to discover. Sleep lightly in your camps: rest not in any single place for long. Remember these conditions and you will live on in this country, through all its dangers, until your hair is grey and you grow taller than the trees.

"As for elephants, count the toes and fingers of all the children here: those whom you have saved. As many toes and fingers as the children have, so you will be rewarded with elephants by the spirits."

There were fifteen children beside the fire. Three hundred elephants sounded good to Bvekenya. He had hardly a shilling of his own left in the world, and the bulk of his belongings had been lost in the fire.

"If I get three hundred elephants, I will be content and leave," he replied.

"You will have them," promised the witch; and all the next day she prayed most earnestly at the burial places of the ancestors and founders of her clan.

Bvekenya prepared to leave. His last night at the kraal was one of the most uneasy he ever spent in the wilds. All night he had strange dreams. He dreamed that he was surrounded once again by police boys. He jumped up and grabbed his gun; but as he loaded it, it broke. He ran, and as he fled he fell into mud; thick, oozy, slimy mud that enveloped him until he was dead.

When he awoke, he expedited his packing and final preparations as much as he could. He was determined to remain no longer in the place. Once before, he had been warned of impending attack and, heedless, had suffered the consequences.

It was only Limbo who delayed him. When he tried to induce the dog to follow him, it refused to budge. Limbo had become a cross between a newly-rich and a miser dog. He had not only gorged himself on meat, but he had sneaked off and buried every scrap of food he could snatch in a hiding place in the bush.

At this cache of food, the dog had taken up permanent residence. He was obviously determined never to be hungry again. He seemed to consider his food stock so big that he could never possibly want; and the saviour of his famine days could now be spurned.

When Bvekenya tried to catch the dog it snarled and snapped.

"All right," he said at last, sucking a bitten hand. "You're certainly a proper newly-rich: you don't want to know an old friend."

He left the dog, sitting snarling on its treasure house of bones. A hyena took it a few nights later. As for Bvekenya, he wandered far and fast; and never afterwards would he sleep in his own hunting camps for longer than a single night, nor did he fail to respond immediately to his intuition, or the strange, secret warnings which came to him from the darkness of his mind.

SIX

The first elephants

From Shubela's kraal, Bvekenya went southwards, back across the Great Save River and into the area in which his Shangane friends had told him he was sure to find elephants.

Two of the Shanganes went with him as guides and carriers, and they soon brought him onto the trail of his first elephant, a sizable bull with a foot twenty-five inches in diameter. The knowledge of being on his first great hunt thrilled Bvekenya. He looked down with fascination at the track, with its complex lines and its telltale shape. In after years, such tracks were to yield a mass of information about the animal at a glance; but to his then inexperienced eyes they meant nothing, save the unmistakably fresh sign of the presence of an elephant.

They soon came upon the animal: too soon, in fact, for Bvekenya. He had hardly made up his mind what to do when they saw the elephant feeding in the mupani forest, breaking branches and munching away at enormous mouthfuls of leaves. The Shanganes nudged him forward. They were very dubious of his ability, and his evident nervousness hardly reassured them.

He advanced towards the animal with great caution, while the Shanganes squatted down on their haunches and watched him in silence. All he knew about hunting an elephant was summed up in the advice somebody had given him to shoot the animal behind the ears. He was hardly happy as he moved forward. More than once he glanced backwards at the Shanganes, but they gave him about as much sympathy as a stone wall.

He stole carefully into easy range. The elephant seemed quite unsuspicious. Bvekenya rested against a mupani tree and took aim. He was only conscious of the beating of his heart. He could hardly breathe. He squinted down the sights, found his mark, and pulled the trigger.

The crash of the shot seemed to shake the trees. There was a thud as the bullet struck, just a bit high. The startled elephant wheeled and hurtled off into the bush. Bvekenya sent two shots into his rear quarters as he ran.

The animal crashed away through the trees. A fainter crashing in the opposite direction indicated the flight of the Shanganes. Their faith in Bvekenya had lasted as far, but no further, than the first fumbled shot.

Bvekenya set off after the elephant on his own. He was determined to get the animal. After the disastrous fire, he was so short of ammunition that he could ill afford to lose the three shots he had already expended. They must have some effect on the elephant in the end, and he was determined to follow until they did.

He took his boots off and tied them around his neck. It was sand country, with no thorns, and he was so hard up that he could no more afford to wear out his boots in a long chase than he could afford to waste the three cartridges.

For five hours, from 10 a.m. until 3 p.m., he tracked the fleeing elephant. He was certain the animal had been wounded, although there were no signs of blood; and when he did catch up with the elephant it was unconcernedly browsing once again in the mupani bush.

Bvekenya slipped up to the animal, and this time got within more than easy range. He was determined not to make a mistake. He lifted the gun and sent three carefully aimed shots into the elephant. The dismayed animal certainly fell this time. Bvekenya was overjoyed. It was his first really profitable kill. In his excitement he put his gun against a tree and ran to the carcass. He could hardly control his joy. Like the merest amateur hunter, he clambered up the elephant's side and danced a jig of joy on its back.

The elephant promptly struggled up. This time it was Bvekenya's turn to hit the ground with a thud, which only differed from the noise of the elephant's fall by reason of his slighter weight.

The elephant was badly stunned. The animal took no notice of the prostrate Bvekenya. It stumbled off like a drunken man, coughing blood, and then fell dead about fifty yards away. Bvekenya danced no jig of joy this time. He watched the elephant for some time before he was certain it was completely dead. Then he advanced cautiously to examine his prize.

There was nothing much to be proud of in this first kill. It had taken six badly placed shots to drop the elephant, and he examined the wounds carefully to determine which had proved deadly. In after years, experience taught him to kill an elephant efficiently with one shot, both mercifully and economically; and he developed astonishing skill in finding the targets of his choice.

The elephant had tusks of smallish size; one of fifty-one pounds and the other (slightly broken) weighing forty-nine pounds. With ivory fetching 8s. 6d. a pound in those days, it meant that his first hunt had yielded £42 10s., and he was reasonably content.

There were no vultures in the area: the drought had driven them off along with the smaller game. In a normal season the vultures could be relied upon to beacon the site of a kill by their presence; but it was obvious that he would have to devise some other scheme of marking the locality before he returned to camp. He solved the problem by simply dragging a stick behind him in the sand as he walked, and this left a clear, easily visible trail.

He spent the night back at his camp, twelve miles away. The Shanganes had been waiting for him when he returned. Their jubilation at the news of the kill was ecstatic. Overnight they gathered the local tribespeople; and with the dawn quite an army of Shanganes made a happy pilgrimage to the site of the elephant's downfall.

For the whole day the place resembled a butcher's shop. The local chief had made a claim for one of the tusks, but Bvekenya brushed him aside. The tusks were his, as well as the first choice of meat and fat. After he and his own followers had taken their pick the rest of the crowd were let loose, and they certainly made astonishingly quick work of the elephant. By evening the carcass had disintegrated until it was just a pile of offal and a stain on the sand.

There was not much chance of the Portuguese police putting in an appearance at so remote a spot, but it was still a possibility. In any case the tusks had to be moved, and for the sake of security the sooner they were moved the better.

Bvekenya applied much thought at various times to the problem of carrying tusks. Tying them on the back of a donkey was no easy matter, for their tapering smoothness always seemed to allow the tusks to slip off.

After much irritating experience, he devised a way of driving wooden pegs into the open ends of the tusks. To these pegs and the tips of the tusks he attached ropes spun from lala palms. The ropes were twisted and knotted at intervals around the tusks. He would then suspend one average-size tusk on each side of a donkey, by means of a loop of rope attached to the coils he had twisted round the tusk.

For really heavy tusks, he devised a variety of sledge made from a pair of poles lashed to the sides of a donkey, with their ends dragging on the ground. A big tusk, or even a full bag of mealies, could be dragged along tied on top of these poles.

Bvekenya carried his first two tusks some twenty-five miles away, to the path along the border. There he buried them at the foot of a baobab tree, so that they would be both secure from any Portuguese raid, and retrievable when it was time for him to return to Makhuleke.

Then he looked for his next elephant, and soon found that one success makes life easier. Instead of having to track an animal down, the tribespeople now came to him and begged that he shoot one old bull who had turned rogue, killed three people (two men and one woman), and generally terrorised the whole countryside.

He had no trouble in finding the elephant. The tribespeople were only too familiar with its track; a big, twenty-eight-inch footprint, as easy to identify with its distinctive scars and markings as a human fingerprint.

Precisely what had turned this elephant into a killer was unknown. He had some grievance against life. Perhaps toothache or ulcers had become too much for him; but at all events he was certainly an unpleasant character. Every human being he had been able to catch on the move he had charged. His technique was always the same. He would spike them on one of his tusks, toss his head to send the body flying, and then trample the victim into a horrible lump of mangled flesh and bone. Like most elephants, he did not like trampling on anyone lying down and keeping still. He liked to catch his victims running. He always covered up the body of his victim afterwards by burying it under the branches he stripped from the trees.

The tribespeople left Bvekenya to follow the trail of the killer, with only his three Shangane followers for company.

It was a long slog through the parched bush. Perhaps they were a bit weary of it all, and half asleep on their feet. Suddenly a bush pheasant sprang up from a clump of grass, screeching its harsh discordant cry of alarm.

The noise certainly woke them just in time. There was a movement ahead. The elephant was standing in dense bush, watching them. The Shanganes and the donkeys scattered, each trying to outpace the other.

Bvekenya steadied his gun. The elephant was already moving towards him. He put a quick shot into the animal's chest, hoping to turn it. The elephant trumpeted, with a blast one could hear miles away. It put its trunk down, folded its ears back, and came for Bvekenya like a tornado, battering every obstruction flat in its path.

Being charged by an elephant, the first or the hundredth time, is not pleasant. Bvekenya had a fleeting impression of birds rising from the falling trees and a pair of alarmed squirrels, one holding a nut in its mouth, scattering for their lives.

Bvekenya jumped sideways and dodged among the trees. He had hardly credited that such a great, lumbering creature could move with such frightening speed. For seventy yards the elephant flattened a trail of destruction through the bush. Then it lost sight of the dodging Bvekenya and stopped uncertainly, dripping blood from its wound and pivoting slowly round, smelling for its quarry.

Bvekenya stopped running as soon as he realised the elephant was still. He sneaked back to a vantage point. From behind a mupani tree, he took careful aim. The bullet hit the giant behind the ear. The reaction was immediate. The elephant dropped straight to the ground, doubled up on top of its own feet.

Bvekenya walked up to the animal. The shot must have killed the elephant instantly, he thought with some satisfaction. At least he was keeping his head and learning.

He shouted for the Shanganes and they came back cautiously, with many an exclamation of wonder as they saw the carcass.

Food was in the air. They busied themselves in lighting a fire, while Bvekenya sat in the shade and indulged in the luxury of a cigar made from leaves and some tobacco he had traded from passing mine labourers. Life was good, and success certainly seemed to be coming his way.

He was half asleep when he heard a startled howl from the Shanganes. The elephant was scrambling to its feet. With a curse, Bvekenya dived for his gun and rammed a bullet into the breech. The elephant was lurching off, banging against the trees on very unsteady feet. Bvekenya ran after it and pumped four quick shots into the elephant from the side. This was the end. The elephant sank down, first to its knees, and then, with a mighty sigh, right to the ground. This time it rose no more.

This second experience of an elephant rising again after it was considered to be dead was never forgotten by Bvekenya. Thenceforth, he always followed the traditional African custom of cutting the tail off a fallen elephant. An elephant had to be very dead before it submitted to the indignity of losing its tail, and possession of this item by the hunter indisputably established proof of ownership. Even if you were forced to leave the carcass for some days and someone else claimed possession, you could always produce the tail, fit it onto its original position, and establish your proper rights.

The killer elephant was certainly a fine big chap, with tusks weighing seventy-five pounds each. It represented £63 15s. in cash to Bvekenya, along with all its meat and fat. The usual feast followed the shooting. The tribespeople had heard the elephant trumpeting and the sound of the shots from afar. They trooped up through the bush with hungry eyes and set to work on the carcass with a will.

Bvekenya buried the tusks close to the path, in a secure hiding place, and went back to the Great Save River. A short rest in the vicinity of water was certainly needed after the exertions of his recent hunts.

He made a camp by the banks of the river, and for the first time in the bush really lived well. His two successes had given him some renown. The tribespeople started to tramp in from miles around, offering to barter small, carefully hoarded quantities of meal and corn in exchange for elephant biltong. He stocked up with a variety of such produce as was available after the drought, and felt more contentment than he had ever so far experienced in life.

There was, however, very little complete relaxation at this Save River camp. He had constantly to be alert in case of an attack, and the mosquitoes were vile. The drought had driven most of those pests out of the bush; but here along the river, though the water made the hot days pleasant, it also brought the mosquitoes at night, and trying to sleep was a misery. Night after night, he spent what would otherwise have been hours of delicious coolness in sitting up swatting the pests, and cursing the fire which had burned his mosquito net.

The Shanganes simply regarded his resistance to the inevitable with wonder. They were aware of mosquitoes, but hardly concerned with them. They had a technique of making a small fire from the leaves of the plant known as *Bhunga Shunu* (stink-away-the-mosquitoes). The burning leaves emitted a hideous stench, insufferable to the mosquitoes but apparently quite acceptable to the Shanganes. The worse the mosquitoes, the closer to the fire the Africans slept. They invited Bvekenya to join them in their odious sanctuary; but between the stench and the pests he was inclined to choose the mosquitoes, and so sat up swatting them for most of the nights.

Like the mosquitoes, game was also plentiful around the pools of the Great Save. At night, particularly, the beautiful forest of towering wild figs, fever trees and other evergreens was alive with a host of animals, preoccupied in the endless process of eating or being eaten.

Bvekenya had some odd experiences along the banks of that river. There were many hippos gathered in the pools; and as it was the season of romance for them, Bvekenya was entertained daily with front-seat views of their behaviour on such occasions.

The big bulls shouted and brawled with one another all through the nights. They waged vicious battles on the mud-banks and in shallow water and even chased one another onto dry land. Their fights were murderous affairs to watch. A pair of rival bulls would often stand up on their hind legs against each other. They would bellow and tear away, ripping the thick skin of their rival open as though they had tusks made of plough-shares. Bvekenya would watch the fights by the hour from the banks. They certainly were diverting entertainment for any spectator. Love, he considered, must be a wonderful thing to make even a fat old hippo perform like that.

On one occasion Bvekenya crossed the Save and went up the banks of its Pembe tributary for a couple of days' hunting. He made a temporary camp at the foot of a small but steep hillock, which had a giant wild figtree growing out of its base and leaning over the river.

Game paths came down to the river on all sides, and one hippo path from over the hillock reached the river right at the camp site. As usual, the hippos were very active that night, grunting and bellowing as they grazed and quarrelled over their love affairs.

Bvekenya lay listening to the noise for some time, until sleep stole upon him with more relentless skill than any predatory animal. He awoke in the early hours of the morning to the noise of a hippo grunting very loudly close to the camp. He looked over the thorn fence, and in the moonlight he could quite easily make out a large animal standing on the path which came down the hillock to the river.

The hippo seemed to be highly incensed. The animal stood grunting its disapproval at the camp in no uncertain fashion. Even the Shanganes were aroused by the noise, which was something, for even the mosquitoes could not spoil their sleep. One of them crawled out of his bed, picked up a smouldering log of wood from the fire, and hurled it at the hippo. There was a thud and a snort of terror. The hippo turned tail and crashed off through the trees, down the steepest slope of the hillock.

Suddenly there was a terrific howl from the hippo. The animal must have struck a patch of gravel. Judging from the noise, the animal had skidded at speed and was tumbling down the hill slope. Bvekenya sat up with a grin and waited for the tremendous splash when the hippo hit the water. Instead there was a crash which shook the hillock, and then such a howl as must have awakened the Shanganes ten miles away.

Bvekenya and his hunters could not make it out. The hippo was bellowing in a continuous blast of sound and making a crashing noise as though he was trying to push a tree down. Unfortunately it was too dark to risk investigating the predicament of an angry hippo at that hour of the night.

They lay in camp, waiting for morning. The noise made it impossible to sleep. With the dawn, they sallied out with their guns to find out what had happened. The hippo was still bellowing, and they had no difficulty in finding him. As they had guessed, the animal had slipped down the steepest part of the hillock. The surprise came when they followed the hippo's further course. He had tumbled over a low cliff, crashed through the top of the giant fig tree, and caught one of his feet in the fork of a branch about twenty feet above the water. There he was suspended, his head just above the water, and the enormous branches of the figtree creaking and groaning in their efforts to support him. Bvekenya shot him in pity, and the Shanganes cut his carcass down with an axe. He was nice and fat, a good prize to get; but all of them agreed that it was a sad end for a hippo.

Listening to the noises of the night was often a profitable occupation. One sleepless night, with hardly a breath of wind, Bvekenya heard the sharp rifle-like cracks of elephants pushing mupani trees down in the distance. He listened closely to the noise, and made his plans according to the way the elephants seemed to be moving.

With the first light, Bvekenya and his hunters were off. Judging from the tracks, there were two elephants grazing together, and they soon overtook them. The elephants were standing in an open glade: one was a thin, lanky animal, about eleven feet high, the other a smaller, tubby individual with insignificant tusks.

Bvekenya set his heart on the lanky elephant, but he was uncertain what to do. Elephants in the open were always dangerous, and this was his first experience of such a hunt. He approached the elephant of his choice with extreme caution and selected his target. If he missed and the elephant charged, he was lost. There was no shelter anywhere. He aimed carefully. As he pulled the trigger the elephant moved. There was a smack as the bullet ripped home, but nowhere near a fatal spot.

Bvekenya stood petrified for a moment. Fortunately, the elephants chose to run. They separated and went off at high speed into the trees beyond the open space. It was a long and arduous chase to catch up. For over ten miles Bvekenya and the Shanganes followed the trail before they found the lanky elephant standing resting in the shade of a tall tree.

It was getting towards evening, and in the dark bush Bvekenya could hardly make out his target. He watched the animal for some time, hoping it would move; but it stood as still as the shadows. Then he decided on a long chance. He lifted his gun and shouted "Hoi!"

The elephant moved its head quickly. Bvekenya seized his chance. He fired at the animal's chest and then jumped for cover in case of a charge. The elephant hardly budged from the spot. The bullet had hit him in the lungs. He smothered where he stood and died without a sound.

The tusks were fair-sized sixty-pounders. Bvekenya was delighted. A month before he had been completely broke. Now he had all the food he wanted, the Shanganes were tremendously impressed by him, and he had some fine tusks.

When the usual crowd of tribespeople filed up, antlike, to dispose of the elephant, he had them cut the tusks out for him and then left them to their feast. With the tusks carried by the donkeys, he set off along the path to Makhuleke, retrieving the four buried tusks as he went and feeling mighty pleased with himself.

SEVEN
A hunter's life

"You've fought a royal combat," said William Pye, looking at the tusks.

Bvekenya was inclined to agree. He was pleasantly engaged in counting the £168 in sovereigns which Alec Thompson had just paid him for the ivory. It was the biggest lump sum Bvekenya had ever received, and the feel of the gold was good.

His return to Makhuleke had been in the nature of a personal triumph. The inhabitants of Crooks Corner had expected nothing further of him save the news of his death. Instead, he had come tramping back into their ragged society, proudly bringing the six tusks as the spoil of his first hunt.

"What happens now?" asked Thompson sitting on the steps of his store, while his Shangane assistants carried the tusks into the storeroom.

"Provisions, cartridges, and a couple of mules," replied Bvekenya, putting his money away.

"And then?"

"Then I'm going back. If that witch was right I've got 297 more elephants to shoot, so you'd better get in a good stock of cash if you want all the tusks."

"And the Portuguese?"

Bvekenya shrugged.

"They can lump it. If that police boy of theirs hadn't raided me I would be far away tip north. Now I'm going to stay just as long as I feel like it."

"They'll get you for it, you know."

"Maybe. But they'll have a run for it if they want to catch me. Before I'm through I'll get back everything I lost, and a hundred times more. And while I'm doing it, when the rains come and it's easier to live, I'll hunt down every one of the devils who attacked me. The Shanganes only understand one sort of justice, and that's rough justice, which is what they're going to get. As for that Folage: when I catch him I'll break his back and let him crawl home along the same sort of path he made me follow."

Pye stared at him curiously. Thompson just shrugged.

"Well, it's your life, not mine; but you're still going to make trouble for yourself. When do you start?"

Bvekenya left two days later, with a good load of food, cartridges, and new camp equipment. Most important of all were his latest acquisitions: two perky little mules – a light-coloured, white-faced animal he named Yapie and used for riding; and a second mule named Witfoot.

Despite the drought, he felt real pleasure this time in going back along the path which held so many evil memories for him. To help him on his way, he now had some success, prestige and experience behind him. He had three good Shangane attendants, an ample supply of food and ammunition, drinking water carried in sealed calabashes slung on sticks over the shoulders of his carriers, and the final luxury of a riding mule.

For the first time he could sit at his ease while he travelled and study his surroundings. The Shanganes followed immediately behind him, and by now he had learned sufficient of their language to understand their conversations and derive infinite amusement from their folklore and naïve observations of the world in general.

As they travelled this afternoon, the Shanganes were deep in argument. One of their notions of life was that every sound had a meaning. They could always interpret the call of a bird, or the roar of a lion, into some odd little phrase or word.

The visit to civilisation, in the rusty shape of the little store at Makhuleke, had been of overwhelming interest to two of the Shanganes, who had never been anywhere nearer the white man's world. While Bvekenya listened, they argued the point about what a cart and horse said, as they had seen and heard one for the first time, clip-clopping along from the store.

The argument kept Bvekenya amused for miles. The third Shangane was more knowledgeable than his two fellows. He had been to the mines and had seen a motor car. A motor car, he informed his fellows with a superior air, said *"Vuka, vuka, vuka"* ("Wake up, wake up, wake up"), when you pressed the starter button on a cold morning. Then, when the engine started, it spoke European language: *"O'right, o'right, o'right* (all right, all right, all right)."

As for the cart, did not *Tsemeli* (the Jackie hangman bird) sit on the trees beside the road and tease the horse by imitating the noise he made with his cart; first in a high-pitched voice: *"Tshiki, tshiki, tshiki"* ("swishing, flicking, wagging your tail").

Then in a deep voice, with a click of the tongue for the "X": *"Xhapha, xhapha, xhapha"* ("clopping, clopping, clopping").

And lastly, in a normal voice, gradually dying away: *"Ziki, ziki, ziki, ziki"* ("going away, disappearing from sight").

They were still arguing when they turned a corner, and suddenly there was an elephant. He was a big and irate bull. He was standing in the path, browsing on a tree. He had been taken by surprise by the party and didn't like it. Neither did they.

There was a scatter into the bush. The Shanganes vanished as though the earth had swallowed them. Bvekenya tumbled off Yapie, the mule, dived for shelter, and rammed a cartridge into his gun. The elephant came down the path like a battleship at full speed. Only Yapie still stood his ground in the path. He looked at the charging elephant and his ears stood up. The Shanganes never had any future argument as to the meaning of the sounds that followed.

"I'll catch you," shouted the elephant, with a blast loud enough to split an eardrum.

"Just see if you can," replied Yapie, in a high-pitched bray.

The mule did an about-turn and went off down the path as fast as the wind. The elephant went headlong after him. As he passed, Bvekenya fired at him: one, two, three, four quick shots. It is odd that it is invariably easier to kill a fresh animal than a wounded one.

The four shots took rapid effect, but the very impetus of the elephant carried him on for a hundred yards, before he collapsed and skidded to a stop that was dead in more ways than one. He was a fine, big chap, with eighty-pound tusks. The mule, however, didn't stop to investigate the mortality. Judging from his tracks, he ran thirty miles without a breather; and then, when Bvekenya eventually retrieved him, he was a changed mule. Ever afterwards, the merest rumour of an elephant was enough to make his ears stand up. He would dig his feet in and refuse to budge a step nearer, and there was nothing they could do to change his mind.

If the mule had learned something of elephants, then Bvekenya, as he shot his first one hundred tuskers in the years that followed, accumulated a vast store of observations, knowledge, and folklore about the animals he hunted.

The big bull that had chased Yapie taught him one lesson. Bvekenya camped close to the carcass, while the local tribespeople cut out the tusks and hacked the animal up into steaks and sausages. By noon of the next day the elephant was a pile of bones left for the hyenas, and the tribespeople trooped over to the camp to thank Bvekenya. One of the men, Zukwa by name, carried with him the elephant's heart on a stick. It was an object of some local wonder, and they wanted Bvekenya to see it. His four bullets had all lodged somewhere in the immediate structure of the heart. The elephant must have been stone dead for a good part of his last hundred-yard chase after the mule.

They buried the two tusks in a hiding place near the path and went on. There was a rumour abroad that a vast number of elephants had collected together in an area about thirty miles south-west of the Great Save River and thirty miles east of the Rhodesian border.

They journeyed through the bush towards the area and soon found the rumours confirmed. In several places they noticed the grass was stamped flat into the ground, as though elephants in immense numbers had congregated there on some occasion.

Bvekenya made his camp and then set out to find the elephants. Njalabane, the headman of a nearby kraal, provided him with the information and guidance he needed. Every year, around December, the elephants collected in this solitary part of the world, the headman told Bvekenya; and that year they were gathering around a shallow, muddy little lake, about six hundred yards by five hundred yards in extent and surrounded by tall thombothi trees.

Led by his guide, Bvekenya made his way to the lakelet. From a distance he could hear the noise of elephants, and he approached the place with as much wonder as caution. The sight was certainly amazing. With the headman, he crawled the last few hundred yards, until the place was in full view.

There were about three hundred elephants gathered in and around the lakelet. They were sporting together, splashing water over one another and were very evidently on a spree.

In the middle of this mass of elephants there towered one enormous bull, completely surrounded by the others but dwarfing them all. From the moment he first saw him, Bvekenya only had eyes for the giant. He was the greatest elephant Bvekenya had ever seen. Njalabane saw his wonder.

"It is *Dhlulamithi*," he said in a whisper, *"The one who is taller than the trees.* He is the mightiest of the elephants in all this land. See his tusks. Behold his size and strength. Truly a chief of elephants, with the cunning of all his ancestors."

Bvekenya's heart ached for possession of the bull. From the distance his tusks seemed so long that they touched the ground as he walked.

Bvekenya searched for a vantage point. Within range of the bull was a tall ant heap. He crept up to it carefully. The wind had dropped and the elephants had no hint of his presence. They splashed and gambolled with one another like children at the seaside.

Bvekenya climbed stealthily up the ant heap. It was a good eight feet high. Just as he reached the top a puff of wind came up. He cursed under his breath, as he realised it was blowing directly from him to the elephants. Their reaction was immediate. If somebody had shouted "shark" to a group of seaside paddlers, it could not have had a more startling effect.

The elephants bolted. Half of them did not know from what they were running. The whole herd splashed through the water and mud, trampling bushes aside and scattering in every direction.

Bvekenya scrambled down the ant heap, still hoping to get in a shot. The move was almost fatal. Half of the elephants seemed to be stampeding towards him. For a moment he was aware of the gigantic bulk of Dhlulamithi bearing down upon him. He dodged behind a thombothi tree, and the elephant veered off. He tried to fire at it, but a younger animal dodged in between and Bvekenya heard the shot slap home somewhere in the smaller elephant's leg. Within a minute the whole herd had scattered in the bush.

Bvekenya returned disconsolate to camp. The memory of Dhlulamithi and his tusks tantalised him. That night, as though to torment him further, the elephants were pushing over trees all around his camp. They were so near that the Shanganes spent most of the dark hours beating on tree trunks with their choppers, trying to drive the elephants away with the noise, in case they trampled over the camp.

Bvekenya longed to pursue Dhlulamithi, but he had a wounded elephant somewhere in the bush and it was his duty to kill it before it turned rogue and vented its rage on the tribespeople.

All the next day, they hunted the wounded animal. They soon found his tracks. The elephant was limping badly. The bullet had actually lodged in one of his leg joints, but he still managed to lead the hunters a long and weary chase.

Eventually, towards evening, they found the elephant hiding in a thicket. Bvekenya ran ahead to the other side of the thicket and left the Shanganes to thump on the tree trunks. The thumping soon flushed the elephant. He hobbled out into the clearing and Bvekenya shot him.

He was only a young elephant, with forty-pound tusks, and Bvekenya was sorry he had to kill him. Given another ten years, the elephant would have been a worthwhile shot.

Now he just represented a poor substitute for the tusks of Dhlulamithi.

Back at the camp, Bvekenya questioned Njalabane about the gathering of the elephants. The Shangane had very definite ideas about the occurrence, and Bvekenya's three hunters sat nodding their heads in agreement at the various points the old man raised.

Each year, according to him, the elephants gathered together during the month of December. The precise rendezvous varied, but it was generally in Njalabane's area.

The elephants did not feed much while they were in the gathering. They would mill around, as though doing a curious, shuffling love dance. Then, as Bvekenya had seen them, they would go and wash together in some shallow lakelet, having great fun and making a loud commotion of trumpeting and stomach rumbling.

The adolescent elephants would then be separated from the adults. In several groups, each escorted by an old cow, very wise in the ways of the bush, they would be led off on a tour, designed to show them all the water-holes, game paths, the best feeding places, and such other points as are of interest to an elephant. This was the teaching of the young elephants, and their final weaning from their mothers. It was the equivalent, said the headman, of the Shangane youths' circumcision guilds and the puberty schools of their girls.

While the young elephants were away, during the month of January, the adults mated. It was that month each year, earlier or later depending on the rains, which the elephants reserved for their love-making.

There was some fighting among the bulls. The big bulls drove the younger, but ambitious, elephants away. Then mates were selected and courtship began. The lovers retired somewhere apart from the main herd. In the shade of some tall tree, perhaps, they would stand for hours, twisting their trunks together affectionately and caressing each other's bodies.

They would go down to the lakelets together and wash each other, sprinkling water and blowing dust over each other's backs and generally being very tender and faithful to their loved one.*

Bvekenya did not like killing an elephant in the month of love-making; but it happened sometimes, and several pairs died happy in the course of his career in the bush.

Once he shot a cow in the early evening. He bivouacked nearby, waiting for dawn. During the night there was a great commotion in the bush. The cow's mate had come and was trying to arouse her. Judging from the tracks, the bull dragged her along the ground for over one hundred yards. Then he went off, collected the herd, and the whole crowd of elephants came and actually tried to lift the dead cow up before the dawn broke and Bvekenya drove them away.

On another occasion he shot two elephant lovers straight in the brain with two accurate shots. There was no blood for the rest of the herd to smell. That night the herd came and rolled and dragged the two bodies for over fifty yards.

Young elephants would often stand around for days trying to rouse their dead parents, while close friends of some stricken tusker would often do their best to drive Bvekenya away in the night, and he would have to chase them off by banging on the tree trunks with an axe.

The love play of the elephants lasted until early in February. Then the old cows brought the young elephants back again to the herd, and by the fifteenth of the month the whole ritual was over. The bulls left the cows for another

---

*An account of a similar gathering of elephants in Zambia may be found in the book *The Hunter is Death* (T. V. Bulpin).

year and roamed off on their own or in small bachelor groups, and the cows were left to attend to the details of their coming confinements in privacy.

Curiously enough, the frequency with which elephants have their young has always been a matter of some dispute among the hunting tribes of Africa. Science tells us that the gestation period is about twenty-two months; but many of the Africans, and not a few of the European hunters, dispute this with the claim that the cows have calves regularly each year.

The Shangane hunters argued about this point among themselves, although on most other matters of observation they entirely concurred. Bvekenya learned much at the fireside gossips he had with the tribesmen and his own hunters. His own observation confirmed most of the things they told him, while even their animal folklore was intensely interesting. The Shanganes were essentially a hunting tribe. Tsetse prevented them from keeping livestock of their own; and all the close study the Africans usually reserve for their domestic beasts was lavished instead on the habits and intimate peculiarities of the wild animals they hunted.

One question Bvekenya raised with them, that night beside the fire, was a matter which had long seemed curious to him. How do hyenas find a dead animal?

Although the country seemed so deserted, every elephant he shot unfailingly attracted hyenas from so many miles away that to put it down to plain scent was hard to believe.

He had particularly noticed the hyenas at the carcass of the elephant which had chased Yapie. By the morning after the kill there were over a dozen hyenas busy disposing of the bones. After he left the site of the carcass he noticed their tracks on the path. Close to the carcass there were the trails of six or seven hyenas.

As he travelled the tracks thinned out, and he could easily see in the soft sand the points at which the different hyenas had joined the path and headed for the elephant. The last hyena trail definitely leading to the elephant had joined the path fully thirty miles away. So how did that animal know of the kill?

The Shanganes had no doubts about the matter. Way up in the sky, so high he appears as just a dot, there flies *Simungu*, the brownish-coloured African hawk-eagle. These birds have cut up the skies into divisions. Like so many separate chieftains, they never intrude in another's area, unless for purposes of definite war against each other.

The hawk-eagles seem always to be on the wing. They are the sentinels of the sky, and their eyes are as searching and probing as an observatory telescope. Nothing escapes them in the miles of bush spread out below. No hunter has a more intent or silent follower than those watchful birds.

The moment an animal is dead the hawk-eagle drops down and goes for the eyes – the only portion which the bird can eat – for the skin of the animal is too tough to open unaided.

The eyes eaten, the bird stakes its claim on the carcass by leaving its droppings on the animal's head. If the droppings are wiped off another hawk is liable to arrive in the other's absence and also stake his claim. A first-class fight follows when the original claim-holder returns.

With these title deeds left behind, Simungu flies off in one direction after another, calling out harshly as he flies away, and then making a curious rattling noise with his wings as he returns to the carcass. Every hyena and jackal within miles hears his cry, for it is meant to attract and guide them to the kill. The bigger the kill, the further the bird flies and the more noise he makes.

Hyenas, said the Shanganes, would even lie on their backs in order to watch the flight of the bird. Time after time, Simungu flies off and returns, settles on the carcass for a minute or so and then rises again and flies off in a different direction. Within hours the hyenas start to troop in.

Simungu then perches on a tree and watches the scavengers tearing up the carcass and laying open the delicate morsels for which he longs. Every now and then he darts in from his perch and snatches up some lump of flesh, in such manner receiving his share of the spoils from those whom he has employed to act as carvers.

After this ingenious answer to his query, Bvekenya rolled over and slept in his camp in the wilds. The bush was silent and peaceful. The great herd of elephants had dispersed fifty miles or more away. Dhlulamithi had eluded him for the present; but sometime, somewhere in the wilderness, he was certain they would meet again.

From the darkness, a hyena began to moan in its melancholy voice. Half asleep, Bvekenya heard his Shanganes chuckle.

"You hear what he says?" said one. "He says 'Mina hamba le' ('I'm going away'). He thinks to cheat us with his voice. Then he will sneak back on his belly to eat the fowls and goats."

Somebody else said something, and the hyena moaned again, further off, alone and far away in the shadows of the night, where Bvekenya hunted Dhlulamithi in his dreams, while he lay and slept in peace and quietness beneath the countless stars.

EIGHT

Trail of the Rain God

W hen the morning came Njalabane awoke Bvekenya.

"Sir," he said. "If you would see game animals and learn of their ways, then we must go together, you and I, to a certain place across the border, there in Bokhalaka (Rhodesia)."

"What is there?" asked Bvekenya, rubbing the sleep from his eyes.

"Sir," said Njalabane, "it seems that the Rain God has walked through the bush there for a short distance; and all the animals have followed in his footsteps, for the grass is green and the leaves are young and fresh. You will see much and hunt well."

"How do you know this?"

"Sir, in the last moon the lightning came, there upon the distant horizon. I beheld *Mangwa* (the zebra). In times of drought he always watches the sky for the lightning of a passing thunderstorm. Mangwa is the cleverest of all the game animals. He is always first in an area of new grass. He reaches it well before the others, who wait to smell where the rain has fallen. But now even *Hongonyi* (the blue wildebeest) has gone, and he is the most stupid of them all. When he can smell new grass, that even I, in the still mornings, can smell the sweetness and the coolness of those places far away where it has rained."

Bvekenya roused himself and broke camp. With Njalabane as his companion, he went westwards through the bush to the Lundi River; and then up along its southern bank to the hippo pools known as Tshipinda, just below the place where the Tshingwesi tributary flows into the main stream of the Lundi.

He made his camp at a place called Mashaka. The local tribespeople confirmed the story of Njalabane. They told him that the rain had fallen and refreshed the country in a narrow belt along the Tshingwesi River, up to the fountain on the rise which they called Matshindo; but which the hunters knew as Jacobsfontein, after a man who had been gored to death there by a white rhino some fifty years before.

All night long around his camp, *Ngululu* (the klipspringer) and *Mbalala* (the bushbuck) whistled and barked at him, while the hippos from the pool grunted as they fed and squabbled in the reeds. It was a warm night – a sure harbinger of a coolish day – and he awaited the coming of dawn with eager anticipation.

Dawn was always beautiful, the best part of the whole day in the wilds. He rose with the first light, stretched himself in the early breezes, the coolest of the day, and made coffee in the embers of the dying fire, the farewell gift of the night before. Then, with Njalabane, he set out to explore the trail of the Rain God.

It was as though the dawn was the doorway through which they had passed from a desert to a garden. For forty miles along the river, in a belt of country little more than three miles wide, the rain had awakened the world to new hope after all the years of drought.

The whole countryside was alive with game animals, feeding on the fortnight-old grass. There were tsetsebe, waterbuck, sable, roan and eland wherever they looked. Ostriches, warthogs and buffaloes were gathered in numbers greater than Bvekenya had ever thought possible. They were on a flat plain, sparsely wooded with mupani trees, which showed off the game to perfection.

Bvekenya's gun was silent that day. All day he walked through that African wonderland, while Njalabane gossiped about the animals and their habits as though they were all old friends.

He saw eight big troops of giraffe alone, while the bird life was so rich and varied that the very air seemed to hum with song.

For the first time, Bvekenya saw a rhino trail and the places where the animal had scattered its dung.

"Look," said Njalabane, pointing out the spots. "This is the wisdom of *Malembe Futsu* (the rhino who eats twigs). He has no tail to drive the flies away; and because they pester him so, he destroys their breeding places by scattering his dung."

Bvekenya questioned Njalabane about this *Malembe Futsu*. He had for long heard of the so-called white and black rhinos, and expected to see two animals of radically different colours. The Shangane knew nothing of this. He was aware of two different species: the *Malembe Futsu*, with narrow mouth, who browsed on twigs; and the *Malembe Mukhombo*, with a wide, flat mouth, who lived on grass but was no different in colour.

Only long afterwards did Bvekenya learn that the name of the white rhinoceros was given as a result of imperfect observation, probably because of an animal daubed with white clay. The old pioneers were responsible for many curious misnomers in Africa. Hyenas were called wolves; leopards were called tigers; and gnus were called wild cattle (*wildebeeste*): so it is not surprising that the myth of the white rhinoceros was readily believed.

Bvekenya was excited to see his first rhinos but from a hunting point of view they were of little value. He encountered a fair sprinkling of those armoured animals at different times in the bush and on one occasion shot a *Malembe Futsu*, but it was hardly worth the cartridge. The meat was as tough as an old trek ox, the skin next to useless for any purpose; and the only item of value was the horn, for which the Indians paid a fair price on account of its use, powdered up, as an aphrodisiac.

All through that first wonderful day, as they tramped through the paradise of animals, Njalabane showed Bvekenya the oddities of the wilds and told him of the secrets of the game animals, which it had taken generations for his people to discover.

"See," he whispered, "there is *Manghovo* (the mongoose) digging for medicine. He has been fighting a snake. He must have been bitten. He digs now for the *sakwakwakwane* shrub, which grows only in this sandy soil. He will dig up a root and eat it. We do the same, for we learn from him. We take the bark from the root and mix it with the venom of a snake. When it is dry and crushed into a black powder we rub it into any snake bite, and drink it as well. It is called *butshungu*, and if you have it no snake, not even the mamba, can ever cause your death."

Lions, leopards, cheetahs and hyenas were all present among the crowds of antelope. Elephants were also there, especially groups of young ones, each led by some weather-beaten and aged cow.

Njalabane imparted more of his old tribal wisdom concerning the customs and habits of the elephants to Bvekenya.

"They, too, have their medicines," he said. "The two-bladed *sheshengwe* leaf which grows so oddly, straight up from the ground, is an especial favourite of theirs. The cows pull it out, chew it and then dose it to the little elephants."

But whether it was taken as a medicine or a refreshment Njalabane was uncertain.

A great favourite in the diet of the elephants is the short *safufanje* grass, while the sweet berries of the marula trees are their greatest annual luxury. When the berries ripen, the elephants will travel ten miles to their favourite trees. They trample the ground smooth beneath the boughs. Then they shake the trees to bring the berries down, blow the berries into a heap with their trunks, and eat them. If the berries are over-ripe and fermented, the elephants will go home singing. All these items are the elephants' delight, but they also have their hates, particularly the black-berried *seshonge* bush. Even one branch of this bush, placed in an elephant's path, will cause the animal to deviate.

With the heat of the early afternoon, Bvekenya and Njalabane rested in the shade of the trees on the banks of the Tshingwesi. The river itself was dry, save for a few disconnected pools; but there was always water buried in the sand a few feet from the surface. They sat in the shadows in silence and watched the game come to drink. They sat so still that one gawky young impala, with its long, graceful neck and its eyes full of the curiosity that lies in its naïve little brain, came right up and stood staring at them in wonder, while *Hlalanyathi* (the oxpecker bird), hung lovingly around its neck, selecting ticks for luncheon with all the care of an epicure; eating the plump ones and leaving the thin ones to fatten.

In the shade of the tall trees the elephants stood and dozed in the heat, swaying gently on their feet and flapping their ears in the warm air to drive the insects away. Cows with young calves to feed are always the thirstiest of the elephants. Each day they go down to drink, leaving their calves behind if they are very small, carefully hidden beneath a pile of mupani leaves. There the calves lie quietly, waiting for their mothers to return; and, like all very young animals, protected by a kindly Providence by having no smell to attract any predatory animal to their hiding place.

Bvekenya watched the elephants in fascination. There was no surface water, so they were digging into the sand of the riverbed like human beings making a well. They carefully trampled the ground firm, to prevent the sand from collapsing as they dug. Then they started to work their trunks into the sand, boring deeper and deeper, until at last they would go down on their knees in order to reach the deepest possible level.

Many of the wells went down as much as eight feet before the elephants found the water they wanted. Young elephants, who cannot reach deep enough, are often forced to swallow sand; and during the years Bvekenya was in the bush he found several of these unfortunate animals dead, as a result of their odd diet.

Like the Bushmen of the Kalahari, the elephants are jealous of their wells. They conceal them carefully after use by burying them with sand, and return time and time again to some favourite well whose water is particularly pleasing.

All afternoon, until the cool of early evening came, Bvekenya and Njalabane watched the animals come down to drink. Then they walked on into the cool shadows which herald the night, and found a fine camping site underneath a tall thombothi tree, which reached up to the heavens from the midst of an old ant heap. At this place they made a circle of protective thorn branches, lighted their fire, and settled down to eat and rest.

It had been a marvellous day. Bvekenya had been so absorbed by all he had seen that never once had he felt any inclination to kill. The place seemed a sanctuary for animals, and the thought of being the means whereby death could find its way to this green paradise was repellent to him.

Yet the grim, primaeval theme of all the wilds – the endless duel between life and death – was being played out all around him. The lions, the leopards, and the lithe cheetahs had of necessity no such scruples as Bvekenya; and in the evening, as he sat with Njalabane at the fire, they heard the far off hunting cry, so cruel and eerie, of *Hlolwa*, the wild dog.

Now in the wilderness there is no one who has anything good to say for *Hlolwa*. Of all wild life, save the crocodiles and snakes, he is the most generally detested.

The lion, the leopard and the cheetah kill their prey as brave men do; but Hlolwa is afraid. He does not like to kill if his prey stands at bay and faces him with courage. A lion will take a chance and fight it out, even with a wounded buffalo. But Hlolwa looks for some antelope: an impala doe heavy with calf, a tiny duiker, or some frightened faun; and then he is in his element.

He loves to put up such a quarry and chase the terrified thing until its heart breaks. He likes to hear it panting and sense its fear: he likes the thrill of a chase which can only have one ending. He likes to eat his quarry while it still runs, ripping at its belly and haunches, feeling the warm blood spurt over his face as he drags the entrails from some heaving flank.

Then, when the animal at last stumbles and falls, he loves to pounce upon it with his piping twitter of excitement. He rips it to pieces with astonishing speed, squabbling with his companions over the juicy bits and wagging his bushy tail in glee. There is marvellous teamwork and cunning in the hunting organisation of a pack. A wild dog hunts well with his fellows; but if one is wounded in the chase, and his blood falls, then his boon companions of the hour will turn and rip him to pieces with as much speed and relish, and as little compassion, as they dispose of any antelope.

Bvekenya had noticed a big pack of hunting dogs among the greenery of the animal paradise. They had been the only living things he had seen that day which he had wished to kill. They were not profitable shots: they possessed nothing of any value; but their very method of killing made others wish to kill them.

They had come up close to stare at him in curiosity, running through the grass with their funny, jumping movement, and standing up on their thin hind legs to peer at him over the grass, their big ears and blotchy white and tawny and black coats making them conspicuous against the young grass and leaves.

He had sent one shot whining through the air at the dogs and they had scattered, twittering at each other in alarm. And now, in the evening, sitting with Njalabane, he heard them hunting in the bush near the camp. The sounds were not far away and were coming nearer. They wondered what unhappy creature was running before the pack, prepared to do anything to escape, even to run beneath a moving wagon or into a kraal; and truly that is the last sign of desperation, for there is seldom mercy in an African hut.

Suddenly there was a crash through the bush. Before they could scramble, startled, to their feet, a kudu cow came hurtling straight towards the camp. Before her was a thick clump of thorns. She sprang straight over, in one magnificent wild leap, and landed spreadeagled hopelessly on top of a second clump, her stomach caught by the branches and her four legs a foot or more above the ground.

In an instant the wild dogs were at her, racing round and round the trapped animal like Red Indians on their ponies, jumping up and snapping at the kudu's legs and flanks, twittering with excitement.

Bvekenya snatched his gun and ran up in a rage. He shot the dogs: one, three, five of them. The rest drew back in sudden dismay. He fired again and they bounded off into the grass, running to a safe distance and then standing up on their hind legs, cursing him in their twittering voices and eyeing their victim and the bodies of their fallen comrades with equal hunger.

Bvekenya ran to the kudu, to try and ease her off the thorns. She lay there and pleaded at him with her big, soft eyes. Her entrails were festooned around the bush like a tangle of rope. The thorns were dripping with blood. Bvekenya shot her through the head as quickly as possible; and then went back to the camp, cursing. Presently the hyenas came and removed the kudu. The wild dogs went off into the night and Bvekenya heard them no more.

With the dawn, necessity turned even Bvekenya into a hunter once again. Meat was the only food he and Njalabane could hope to find in the game area, for there were no kraals for many miles. Bvekenya was loath to disturb the herds of antelope, but it had to be done. At least, he decided, he would select only one large animal; and its meat, dried into biltong, would last them for some time.

Bvekenya had noticed several herds of buffalo the previous day, and he was tempted to shoot one, for they were large animals and, as he had not shot one before, its meat would be a novelty to him.

With Njalabane, he walked down into the dry bed of the river and made his way through the reeds, searching for a herd of buffalo. There was little game in the thick reeds and river shrubs. Game animals prefer to be in open country, where the cooler winds can reach them, and where they have a better chance of both seeing and smelling an enemy. Only in time of danger do they seek sanctuary in the thickets; and then, especially where buffalo are concerned, they can be at their most dangerous.

Njalabane had warned Bvekenya of the danger of *Nyari*, the buffalo. An elephant, with his deceptively kindly face, can lull you into a sense of security until you look into his eyes: tiny, red eyes, full of secret thoughts and hates and rages. But at least when an elephant loses his temper, he soon recovers it. Within a few minutes the storm has passed, and if you have escaped the first sudden fury you are reasonably safe. But when *Nyari*, the buffalo, loses his temper he seldom finds it again; and for a long time life in his vicinity can be unpleasant.

For some time, Bvekenya and Njalabane hunted along the river without finding a buffalo. Then they separated, each searching in a different direction. Soon afterwards, Bvekenya stumbled upon a medium-sized herd, drinking at a pool which lay surrounded by tall, isolated boulders.

The herd scented him almost as soon as he sighted them. They stampeded for the reeds: a rush of thundering hoofs and brownish animals, shouldering one another out of the way in their panic. Bvekenya ran and clambered up to the top of one of the boulders. The boulder was a massive lump of sandstone, firmly wedged into the river bed, lifting its rounded top some nine feet above the ground.

From his vantage point on the boulder top, Bvekenya could look down onto the reeds. He soon saw the herd bull, a young animal with more temper than sagacity. The bull was nosing around in the reeds, trying to smell Bvekenya; but he was somewhat confused in his orientation by the irregular puffs of wind.

Bvekenya shouted, to confuse the bull still further. In a rage, the animal started hustling about in the reeds, sniffing the air and trying to see its unknown enemy. In this way, the bull at last worked his way downwind from Bvekenya. He immediately got the scent and swung round facing the boulder. With a snort he half charged up towards Bvekenya, and then paused, obviously very uncertain what to make of the rock with the human being perched on its top.

Bvekenya waited for the bull to come into range. When it did, he picked his shot and fired. The buffalo leaped into the air with a cow-like bellow as the bullet slapped into him.

He came down solidly on his four legs with a grunt, put his head down, and tore through the reeds like a battering-ram.

Bvekenya hastily lifted his legs. The bull hit the boulder with a thud that must have shaken his teeth loose. He drew back in amazement, tossing his head to collect his scattered wits. Then he tried again. This time he hit the boulder with enough force to shake it.

Sitting straddled on the top, Bvekenya felt a sudden pang of alarm. But he need not have worried. That last charge was the buffalo's Waterloo. He had knocked himself silly.

The bull slid down backwards on his haunches and struggled groggily to rise again, while Bvekenya stared down in wonder into his dark eyes. Then the bull keeled over with a grunt and died. Bvekenya's bullet had passed through the bull's stomach; and that, combined with the two tremendous cracks on the head, was the death of him. There was a great frying of buffalo kidneys in Bvekenya's camp that night.

For over a month, Bvekenya and Njalabane remained in the trail of the Rain God. Then the time came for them to go back to the wilderness, and on the last night Bvekenya sat down beside the campfire and wrote a letter. During all the time he had been in the wonderland of game animals, he had longed intensely for the companionship of someone of his own kind, who would share his appreciation of the wonderful scenes around him. For the first time in the wilds, he had felt a pang of loneliness. There was no European within a hundred miles of him.

He had seen the name and address of the nearest Rhodesian authority on the official documents of the tribespeople. Accordingly, it was to this authority, P. Forrestal, the Native Commissioner of Chibi in the Fort Victoria district of Southern Rhodesia, that Bvekenya addressed his letter, in order to unburden his heart to one of his fellows.

He sealed it up, and some days later gave it to a Shangane, who told him that he was walking to Chibi in search of work. Bvekenya saw the man off, with his letter carried in a small forked stick to save it from being soiled by handling. He had little hope of the letter ever being safely delivered; but six months later a reply duly reached him, carried laboriously through the bush by how many different hands he could not guess. Like his own letter, the reply was kept in a forked stick, and the envelope was clean.

Bvekenya opened the envelope eagerly, and in the shade of a mupani tree sat down to read its contents. It was dated June, 1914.

"Dear Barnard,

Your letter from your happy hunting grounds, dated three days after the second new moon of 1914, is to hand. It is certainly very interesting and instructive.

"I did not know that elephants go through the process of weaning and instructing their calves in the way you mention. Nor did I know that they eat the bones of dead elephants (just as cattle eat the bones of their own kind). This, of course, explains why the skeletons of elephants are never found, and doubtless gave rise to the myth of the elephants' secret graveyard.

"The rhino you refer to as having a narrow mouth is the black rhino, and the animal with the wide and flat mouth is the so-called white rhino. As you say, there is no difference in their colour. I am pleased to learn that we still have both varieties left in Rhodesia. I hope they won't be destroyed in time, as you say.

"I quite agree with you, that the part of the world which you are in would make an excellent game reserve, but I don't think our authorities will move in this direction. All our game is at least legally protected already, although I gather that you don't realise this!

"I don't agree with you that we should make roads through your animal paradise and connect it up with the game reserve of the Northern Transvaal and invite tourists to see the game. As you say, there would be thousands of visitors and we would require a guard for every visitor.

"I will, however, forward your letter to the proper authorities.

Yours faithfully,

P. Forrestal."

Bvekenya read and re-read this letter in the days that followed, until it fell to pieces and the contents were graven on his memory, word for word. It was but a small thing – a solitary letter – but somehow or other it was like the hand of friendship extended to him by one of his own kind across all the miles of bush and wilderness, through all the solitude and loneliness which lies in the vast spaces of Africa.

NINE

The vengeance of Bvekenya

Bvekenya was impatient for vengeance. It rankled in his mind to know that the people who had raided him were still untouched, for rumours had filtered through the bush that many of those concerned were openly boasting of their participation in the affair, and jeering at him as a person of little consequence or courage.

He had intended waiting for the rains to come before he indulged in vengeance, for it was essentially a luxury, to be enjoyed when he could afford the time from his struggle to keep alive and rehabilitate his fortunes. The rest and plenty in the path of the Rain God, however, had turned his mind to thoughts of adventure and revenge.

Most of the raiders had come from Garakwe's village, about fifty miles north of the Save. Bvekenya made his way towards this place, sending a fringe of spies ahead of him, in the persons of those Shanganes who had become his friends and allies.

Through these spies, he gathered all the information he wanted about the village. He had no desire to involve his own Shanganes in the coming fight, although they were willing enough. Vengeance must come from himself alone. If he was to remain in the bush for all the future years of hunting he had planned, it was necessary that he establish a reputation with the tribesmen as a man who would not suffer interference from anyone, at any time. Besides, he had anticipated retribution for so long that the thought of personally encountering each single one of the raiders had become a prospect of delight.

Thus it was, at dawn one morning, while his Shanganes squatted in the bush behind him, that Bvekenya strode into Garakwe's village, with a revolver, his two fists and a sjambok as his allies.

A woman, coming outside at dawn to scratch herself, saw him first. She literally howled a warning. The kraal awoke in a flurry of panic. Nobody knew by what force they had been attacked. Some of the villagers escaped by pushing holes through the backs of their huts. Others stormed their way through the narrow entrances, the men trampling the women and children down in the panic and racing off into the bush.

Bvekenya's spies had told him which of the huts contained the village headman. He made his way straight to the entrance. He felled the first man to crawl outside with a crack on the head from his sjambok handle. The headman was already halfway out before he realised what had happened. Bvekenya seized him by the scruff of his neck, jerked him upright, and gave him a smack on the jaw which made him sleep more soundly than he had during the night before. The rest of the hut's occupants were frantically digging at the back of the structure, trying to force an emergency exit. Bvekenya left them alone. Two men were enough for the present. He fired a couple of shots from his revolver to add extra speed to the flight of the villagers, and then turned on his two captives.

He had anticipated his vengeance for so long that he followed a carefully prepared routine, subsequently famous as Bvekenya's "culture of the bush". He forced his half-conscious captives into a sitting position, with their arms around their knees. He tied their wrists together with thongs and then pushed sticks under both men's knees, in such a way that the prisoners were made to lean over their own arms and were kept hopelessly, and permanently, in a sitting position.

At Crooks Corner, he had first heard the ancient theory that the reason God in his wisdom had created the hippopotamus in every area occupied by the black man was to provide sjamboks with which to thrash him. The sjambok Bvekenya carried with him was of hippo skin, very supple, with a cut like a knife.

When he had finished he left the men whimpering on the ground, in a muddy mixture of their own blood, sweat and tears. Both had admitted participation in the raid and given him much information concerning the whereabouts of the rest of their fellows. Both acknowledged Folage as the leader; but he was far away at the Portuguese post of Massangena, and it would take patience and guile to effect his capture. The second in command had been a certain Khambanyane, a professional footpad whose whereabouts was always uncertain, but who generally lurked on the paths, robbing returning labourers from the mines.

Bvekenya explored the deserted village. He found a few of his former belongings in one or two of the huts, but it was a poor sort of place. He intended to make it poorer. He dragged his two victims to a position where they would be warmed, but not quite cooked, and then set the village on fire. It burned well.

He left the place still alight and went back to his hunters, sitting in the bush watching the smoke of the village curling to the skies. He told the Shanganes what had happened and discussed the next move with them.

He had quite a number of addresses to visit. For the next few months he was a very unwelcome visitor at many kraals. Always his technique followed the pattern of his culture of the bush. There was the careful spying out of the land, followed by a surprise visit from Bvekenya on his own. An occasional fight took place if somebody tried to resist him, and quite a few individuals had their teeth knocked out; but there was never any very resolute mass opposition. The usual tying up, thrashing and burning of huts ended the visitation.

The path of vengeance took Bvekenya many miles. His attackers had scattered after the fight on the Save, and scattered still further when rumour reached them of what was happening. The culture of the bush was a form of tuition hardly of the postal variety, and those Shanganes with a guilty conscience did their best to become individuals of very uncertain address.

It was surprising how quickly, and how far, the stories of Bvekenya's vengeance spread through the bush. The most sensational details were carried to the Portuguese and Rhodesian authorities of Bvekenya shooting tribespeople and tying up obstreperous pupils of his culture to be toasted before some slow fire, to give them time for thought and subsequent sorrow.

The official hair stood on end in both Rhodesia and Mozambique at these lurid tales. Warrants for arrest were issued with a promptitude more notable in drafting than execution. The Rhodesian warrants on charges of assault with intent occasioned Bvekenya some slight regret. It was true that he had caught and thrashed a few of his attackers who had fled over the border to Tshisa's kraal, between the junction of the Lundi and Save rivers; but his complaints were essentially with the Portuguese Shanganes.

The Portuguese had warrants for assault with intent, poaching, illegal entry, and half a dozen other interesting complaints. They were of little real interest to Bvekenya. A sentence of twenty-five years in gaol, passed on him *in absentia* by the Portuguese, sounded impressive; but they would still have to catch him, and the bush was vast.

Towards the end of his campaign, he was reasonably satisfied that the bulk of his attackers more than regretted their indiscretion. Only Folage and Khambanyane still awaited his tuition, but their turn would certainly come. For the present, it was time for him to return to Crooks Corner. By then he had been out in the bush for a long time, and his supplies, ammunition and equipment needed replenishing. He had been hunting as well while he took his revenge, and he had ivory to sell.

There had been some changes since Bvekenya first visited the store of Makhuleke. Alec Thompson had sold the store to Jack Ford and left Crooks Corner for parts unknown. Replacing him as manager of the ramshackle establishment was a lanky, fair-haired Canadian named by his parents Dorlon Thomas Buchanan, but known to his customers by the more familiar name of Buck.

Just why Buck Buchanan had found his way to this warm corner of the world from the snowy prairies of his own country remains unknown. He had come out to South Africa in 1897, escorting a cargo of donkeys sent as a relief measure after the rinderpest had wiped out most of the country's draught animals. After drifting around Southern Africa for some years, he had at last cast his anchor in the stagnant waters of Crooks Corner. He and Bvekenya became firm friends, for he was a congenial character, fond of reading, and always with plenty of time on his hands to yarn with any stray visitor. His normal day's work commenced an hour before dawn, ended just after sun-up, and then degenerated into the usual day-long hunt for shade common to all the odd folk at Crooks Corner.

Bvekenya had no need to introduce himself to Buchanan. Exaggerated stories of his hunting adventures and the culture of the bush had spread his fame, so that he was rapidly becoming the star character of all the customers at Makhuleke.

Buchanan had much gossip of interest to Bvekenya. Among the items retailed to him in the shade of the trees around the store was the news that Khambanyane, the much sought-after second in command to Folage in the fight on the Save, was a visitor in Crooks Corner. Furthermore, the gentleman was inclined to be boastful. He was staying in the kraal of Makhuleke himself; and every time he came to the store he regaled the customers and loafers at the place with fresh details of how he had personally beaten up Bvekenya.

The news rankled with Bvekenya. He badly wanted to interview Khambanyane, but he had long hoped that by the exercise of some discretion he might keep his name clean with the Transvaal police and always know that at his base at Makhuleke he could find a sanctuary, without fear of raids or official persecution.

Accordingly, he held his peace for a few days. To thrash Khambanyane in Transvaal territory would be hopelessly compromising, and yet the presence of the man was irritating. The local Shanganes eyed Bvekenya quizzically, and the loafers at the store always seemed to find some joke at which to snigger every time they saw him. He could guess that they were gibing at his peaceful acceptance of the presence of Khambanyane. He could guess, as well, that Khambanyane was fully exploiting in his stories the lack of any obvious reaction to his taunts.

Bvekenya stood the sniggers for five days. Then he went to Buchanan.

"I've stood it for five days too long," he said in disgust. "I'm just not made that way. Here, keep me out of temptation. Look after my gun and sjambok."

"What now?" asked Buchanan, stowing the weapons away beneath the counter. "You turning to religion?"

"No, to my fists. That fellow might be able to run to the police with sjambok scars and they'd have an assault charge;

but if I just give him a good hiding, man to man, that might settle the account and give me a lot of satisfaction."

Buchanan was dubious.

"I dunno," he said, scratching his bristles. "A hiding's a hiding, whichever way you get it. And he's a big bloke, that Shangane. You reckon you can handle him?"

"I mean to," said Bvekenya over his shoulder, "but don't you come, otherwise you might get pinched as a witness, and that would be awkward."

He walked down the ridge from the store whistling. He felt like somebody who had just paid the last instalment on a pawnbroker's loan and bought his self-respect back. A crowd of small Shangane boys guessed his intentions and filed along behind him on the pathway. He could hear them making wagers on the outcome of his visit as they followed him.

Makhuleke's village was a fair-sized establishment of its kind. There were a dozen or more huts collected around one, which, from its size and the number of beer pots standing outside, indicated its importance as the residence of a chief. Makhuleke himself was an old rat of a Shangane, soaked in liquor.

Bvekenya walked into the village, still whistling. A crowd of men were sitting in the courtyard of the chief's hut enjoying themselves with a friendly mixture of beer, quarrelling and conversation. They stared at him in sudden silence as he pushed his way into the place.

"What is it?" mumbled the chief.

"Is the beer good?" asked Bvekenya pleasantly.

"Certainly," said the chief, half confused. He pointed doubtfully at a big pot, containing a mixture of beer, scum, and drowned flies. Bvekenya stooped and picked up the pot. The Shanganes stared at him in silence. Khambanyane was still wiping the froth from his lips after his last drink.

Bvekenya raised the pot with almost a sigh. It was a hefty three gallons of beer. He lifted it above his head and threw it straight at Khambanyane. The pot disintegrated on the man's head.

For a moment there was silence. It was broken only by the dripping of beer down Khambanyane's body and the clamour from the urchins outside, protesting because they could not see what was happening in the courtyard.

Then Khambanyane rose with a splutter. The rest of the Shanganes made a dive for the entrance. Whatever happened now was a matter between Bvekenya and his enemy. Anybody else was distinctly superfluous. They were all afraid they might be involved in the affair as witnesses. Contact with the police in any way was repugnant to the folk of Crooks Corner. It could always lead to their being investigated themselves.

Khambanyane came at Bvekenya with a rush. He was a big chap, about Bvekenya's weight; and, by the look of his scars, well experienced in battle. He was still dripping with beer, and a part of the clay pot seemed stuck in his skull.

Bvekenya met him halfway. He let drive with a kick in the loins that lifted the man an inch in the air. Khambanyane went down with a howl. He twisted on the ground, his face contorted with a mixture of pain and rage. Bvekenya wanted a chance to jump on the man's face, but he squirmed out of the way like a snake.

From the ground, Khambanyane seized the rim of a beer pot. He whirled it into the air with the full sweep of his arm. It looked like a comet with a tail of beer. Bvekenya ducked, but the pot hit him a glancing blow on the top of his head. It sailed off over the reed screen of the courtyard and hit a treetop, with a crack that sent a shower of beer to earth like a drunkard's dream of raindrops.

Bvekenya was half silly from the blow. Khambanyane's head must have been solid bone to stand a full-scale blow.

In his daze Bvekenya saw the Shangane reach for a second pot. He dodged that one by falling to the ground. The pot tore a hole through the fence and vanished outside.

It was Bvekenya's turn now. There was no shortage of beer. The women must have been busy brewing for weeks, preparing for some drunken feast. He grabbed two pots in quick succession and hurled them at the Shangane. Khambanyane dodged the first by twisting his head, but the second landed squarely on his chest. The beer half drowned him. He kicked around, gasping, overturned a few pots, and then scrambled up.

Both men were now on their feet, on opposite sides of the courtyard. For the next two minutes beer pots flew. The air reeked with the stuff; the ground was a soggy mess. If there were any earthworms they would be drunk for a month.

Twice Bvekenya hit his target with pots and jars, and missed with eight more. Khambanyane threw them as though firing an artillery barrage. One connected and half dislocated Bvekenya's shoulder. Over a dozen more missed. The sudden pain of the blow was the last straw for Bvekenya. He dodged a pot and rushed at the Shangane. The man came to meet him, and Bvekenya slipped in the beer. The Shangane caught him around the shoulders in a claw-like grip, digging his fingers into Bvekenya's shoulderblades. For a moment Bvekenya stared into his face. Then he brought his head down with all his force. It felt as though he had hit his head on an anvil. The Shangane received the blow full on the mouth. Bvekenya heard his jawbone snap.

Khambanyane released his grip with a gasp. As he did so, Bvekenya stepped back and slammed in a roundhouse right that sledge-hammered the Shangane across the courtyard. He crashed into the screen and collapsed onto the floor in a mixture of reeds and beer.

Bvekenya went and looked at him. He was not dead, but his injuries looked as though they would stay with him until he died. He was completely out for the count. Hitting him again would be a waste of effort. Bvekenya picked up the last pot of beer and dumped it on the man's head as a parting gift.

Then he went outside. The top of his head felt three times too big. Blood was running down his face, and his clothes were caked with mud and beer. There was not a soul near the kraal. A few fowls and one dog were drinking the beer, which was still trickling from the courtyard. A couple of the hens already seemed a bit top-heavy, and a rooster was crowing happily. Bvekenya left them to their party and went back to the store.

Five days later, he packed up his belongings and left once again for the bush. For the time being, at least, he had had enough of vengeance. On the path, just across the Limpopo, he found two kudu bulls lying dead, with their horns locked together. They had fought once too often for the love of a cow and had died miserably of starvation when they could not disentangle their horns.

Bvekenya took the sight as an object lesson. He remembered Buchanan's voice as he had dressed the wounds on his head.

"You've sure had your vengeance, fellow, but it's cost you something."

Bvekenya agreed. His head ached for a month. As for Khambanyane, as soon as he had recovered, he took himself and his scars off to the nearest Transvaal police post at Sibasa. There he told his lugubrious tale to the interested sergeant. The result was the usual warrant for Bvekenya's arrest, on a charge of assault with intent.

He heard about the charge long afterwards, by rumours passed through the bush. There was nothing very unusual about such charges by then. The new one was awkward, in so far as it now meant that everybody wanted him. Crooks

Corner was a sanctuary only on account of its conveniently mobile border beacon.

Beyond that, it was a matter of those who wanted him having to come and find him. It promised to be an interesting and lively search. He wondered at times who would be the first to try, and wished them luck, for they would certainly need it.

If his career of vengeance had embarrassed his reputation out of the bush, it had certainly given him security at home. The Shanganes behaved as obsequiously as whipped curs. At every kraal he passed the people fawned on him, shouting his praises because of his gifts of meat and the renown of his strength and adventures.

It looked as though he had defeated one enemy, but at the cost of making three more. Henceforth, he could walk in security among the bush Shanganes but must live in alarm at the prospects of a raid from the police. He considered the matter as he followed the path. It really did not make much difference. The old witch at Shubela's had warned him to live on his wits and always be wakeful, expecting anything that came his way and being prepared to meet it.

There was nothing unusual about that way of life. Every animal, bird and insect in the bush, man included, lived in perpetual alarm. Every day and every dark night held its terrors: new enemies to outwit and strange alarms to confront. The wild creatures lived by their fangs and their claws and the strength of their wings. He would live by the strength in his heart and the speed of his gun. Let those who wanted to come and get him if they could.

All he wanted was the freedom of the bush and the vast spaces; an open pathway to the elephant grounds, where Dhlulamithi roamed with the three hundred tuskers the witch had promised him; and a chance of meeting Folage somewhere in the wilds and breaking his back with a crack like the crack of the trees the elephants pushed over in the quiet of the night.

TEN

The camp by the Tshefu

vekenya's happy hunting ground was the wilderness which lay between the Great Save and the Limpopo rivers. Occasionally he strayed beyond the confines of this area of solitude and bush; but it, above all others, was the favourite grazing ground of the elephants, and as such it was Bvekenya's natural home.

In the course of his years in this chosen hunting ground, he grew to know every bend and rise of the pathways which criss-cross the place. Just how many thousands of miles he tramped along those paths he never knew. With his Shanganes carrying a few calabashes of drinking water, some salt, sugar and ammunition, he would lose himself in the bush for months on end, and hunt.

Apart from ammunition, he could be completely independent of the outside world. For food there was venison and the wild berries and roots. He wanted few luxuries. Coffee he made himself, from the roasted and ground up seeds of the baobab tree. If there was anything else he wanted, he could send a messenger to the nearest store – Ballantyne's store at Mount Selinda in Rhodesia, 150 miles away.

Of course, he could not live entirely by restlessly wandering around. It was necessary, and desirable, that he find some central depot in the wilderness, if only to enjoy an occasional rest: some spot made congenial to his needs and nature because of its seclusion, security and situation, as pleasant as one could hope for in this wasteland of sandy flatness and tangled bush.

In such a way did Bvekenya's camp by the banks of the Tshefu River come into being. The Tshefu is a small river, insignificant on the map; but in its pools there is always water, and along its banks stand tall and shady trees. It is remote and lonely, isolated in miles of forest country, sparsely inhabited by any human beings, but ever a special resort of bull elephants.

At a place known as *Mazimbe* (the name of a Shangane who had died there) Bvekenya made his depot in the bush and established both a holiday resort and a variety of manufactory. It was not only ivory which was of value to the professional hunter; the making of whips and sjamboks from the hides of game animals was also extremely profitable.

Bvekenya would hunt for a while, making biltong from the fallen animals and collecting their skins. These skins would be soaked in a mixture of a spoonful of arsenic to ten gallons of water, in order to preserve them from parasites. Then, when a quantity had been collected, Bvekenya and his Shanganes would retire to Mazimbe, and for weeks on end they would be busy working on the skins.

The branches of all the tall trees would be festooned with thongs. The long strips of green leather would be suspended from the branches, with heavy logs tied to the lower ends to stretch them down. A stick would be passed through the thongs and the Shanganes would wind the thongs round and round, like sailors turning a windlass, until they were twisted up into springy lumps which would spin round and round the moment they were released. Over and over they would repeat this winding, until the thongs were pliable and soft.

Giraffes yielded the best wagon whips. There were numbers of these gawky animals scattered in the bush of Bvekenya's hunting ground. Many a time he had great chases after them, galloping through the low bush on a horse skilled in dodging its way past the trees, while the giraffes, with their long legs, stepped high over all obstructions and raced on straight ahead.

A big giraffe yielded over 100 wagon whips, each 15 feet long; and they fetched good prices. The best all-round whips came from the sable, as its skin was of just the right thickness and shape. A big sable yielded 25 whips, skilfully cut from the neck to the front hoofs and from the bottom of the hind legs up.

Buffaloes, numerous at all the rivers, yielded excellent boot leather; while the hippos, found particularly in the pools of the Great Save, were the traditional source of sjamboks. Prices varied around six shillings a whip; but a good, genuine sable whip would fetch at least 7s. 6d.

Life in the camp on the Tshefu was a pleasant change from the hardship and constant travel in the bush. Bvekenya and his Shanganes worked at the skins, but they also rested. Without thought of bilharzia, they swam in the pools of the river; rigged up calabashes with holes in the bottoms in the trees, to act as shower-baths; lived well on wild fruits and biltong; and generally had a thoroughly lazy and enjoyable time. A few odd experiences also came their way and helped to keep things lively.

One evening, while they were just dozing off, they heard a sudden commotion. Each man sat upright in his bed and listened. There was a strange sound coming from the bush around the camp: a sound of something thumping against the trees, just as they sometimes thumped to frighten elephants away.

It was an eerie, uncanny sound, moving from one tree to another all around the camp.

"We are bewitched," suddenly quavered the voice of one of the Shanganes. "It is the ghost of Mazimbe come to drive us away.

To say that his companions agreed with him was putting it mildly. There was a rush for the nearest trees. Pots, fire and belongings were all upset in the panic. The terror was infectious. They scrambled up the tree trunks like startled squirrels.

From his perch on a bough, Bvekenya listened to the noise in bewilderment. The Shanganes were almost weeping with fear. The thumpings went on at intervals for hours. Then the noise gradually died away: bump, bump, bump, into the distance. Nobody moved from the treetops until dawn.

When the light came they all climbed down to the ground again with stiff legs and sore backs. They examined the camp. They found that one of their storage tins, containing the fat they used in dressing skins, was missing. All around the camp was the trail of a hyena.

They tracked the animal down. It was easy to see what had happened. The hyena had got his head jammed in the tin of fat. He had run about all night, bumping into trees. They followed his erratic course with wonder. He had eventually rammed the tin into the fork of a tree and become wedged.

All signs pointed to a mighty tug of war. The hyena had put himself into reverse and practically dug himself in. Something had to give, and it was half the fur from the hyena's head. He must have come out with a pop. The place where his buttocks had hit the ground was still clearly visible. Not that the hyena had stopped to look. He had bolted, leaving the tin in the tree. It was a sheepish-looking crowd of hunters who went back to the camp.

Hyenas were a great plague around the camp. They played havoc with the skins and whips. Traps were set to catch them, but they were cunning brutes and enormously strong. One hyena raided the camp at night and seized a big bundle of thongs. On his way out with his booty, he put his foot in a trap. This hardly deterred him. The trap was attached to a sizable log of wood, but he dragged the whole affair, along with the thongs, for three miles through the bush.

Then he managed to wriggle his foot out of the trap, and off he went to enjoy what was presumably a tasty banquet of thongs.

Lions also came to the camp, although the attraction for them lay in the mules and donkeys. Poor old Yapie (of elephant fame) seemed to be a particularly tasty target for attack. Twice the lions tried to get him while he grazed in the bush. Both times he kicked himself free, but the scars on his sides revealed just how narrow were his escapes.

The donkeys were the worst sufferers from the lions. One night the lions got two of them. Bvekenya was annoyed, for the donkeys were good workers and indispensable to his plans. He left the two half-eaten carcasses lying in the bush and thoughtfully placed a large open calabash of water next to them.

The lions came back again that night. They must have been pleasantly surprised at the hospitality of man. First donkeys were provided (and lions were always uncommonly partial to donkeys); and now water was served to quench their thirst. They dined well and then took long drinks. The next event was even more unexpected – a hearty stomach ache; and by dawn two of the lions were stretched out cold from the strychnine in the water.

When the donkeys were released to graze in the bush the usual clapper bells were tied around their necks, in order to facilitate finding them again. The lions apparently regarded these bells as dinner gongs, for wherever the donkeys tried to hide, their bells naturally gave them away.

Since his experience with Limbo the newly-rich, Bvekenya had acquired two dogs. Of these, one was a sort of Irish terrier. He was named Mac and he was a dog with a great sense of fun. He was always teasing someone, grinning with humour at the scares and misfortunes of others; but not too good, sometimes, at taking jokes himself.

Mac was always intensely amused at the donkeys and their bells. They provided him with permanent entertainment. He would be lying down dozing in the camp, everybody stretched out on their backs in the shade and only the buzzing of the insects or the chatter of the cheeky, glossy starlings perched in the trees above (nicknamed bush baptists from their habit of "baptising" all and sundry with their droppings) to disturb the heat of the day. Suddenly, from the distance, there would sound the faint clang of a bell.

Up would go Mac's ears. A light would come into his bored eyes. Then off he would go on a merry chase through the bush; the yelp of his bark and the clang of the bell gradually fading into the hum of the insects and Bvekenya's drowsy "Drat that dog" as he turned over on his other side.

Hours later Mac would return to camp, hot and blown but grinning with delight. He would expertly dodge any boot thrown at him and then sit down to rest, his tongue hanging out and his thoughts far away on the chase.

Once they were packing up camp and preparing for a fresh hunt. The bells were always taken off the donkeys when they were rounded up and burdened with their loads. The bells had been thrown down in a pile on the ground, preparatory to being packed up. With a silly grin on his face, Mac picked one of the bells up from the ground and walked around the donkeys shaking it.

"All right, Mac," said Bvekenya. "You asked for it."

He called the dog over and tied the bell around its neck. The Shanganes stopped loading and watched with a grin.

Bvekenya suddenly let the dog go and gave him a smack on his haunches. Mac moved off a step, shook himself, and the bell rang.

He was off like a shot. He hurtled through the bush with his tail between his legs, the bell clanging madly. The laughter in the camp died away. The Shanganes ran after the dog, calling him back; but the sound of the bell moved off further and further into the bush. Within a couple of minutes the sound had vanished into the distance.

The matter was now no longer a joke. Cursing, they off-saddled, unpacked their goods, and made their camp again. Then they set off in different directions, to find the dog. Kraals scattered in the bush up to twenty miles away were visited and enquiries were made; but nobody had seen or heard of Mac.

For three days they searched for the dog. Then they gave him up for lost. If he had not gone mad or died of thirst, then some hyena must certainly have caught him. They broke camp once again and set off for the hunting grounds.

They were about seven miles away from the camp when they heard a bark. Unmistakably it was Mac's bark. They called, but he would not come. They listened carefully and could hear the bell.

They went through the bush in the direction of his bark. Mac had the last laugh. He had cornered ten eland cows and their calves. He was walking around and around them, ringing his bell and hemming them in against a dense clump of bushes, while the great, hulking animals stared at him in stupid fear.

If one eland tried to break away, he would dash off and round it up. The grass had been trampled flat all around. Both dog and elands looked lean and famished. For probably the whole three days Mac had kept the elands cornered, allowing no grazing or drinking, and taking no rest, food or water himself.

Bvekenya called him, and he ran laughing into his master's arms. They fussed over him, took off his bell, gave him water and food, pitched a camp, washed him, and then sat around patiently waiting while he slept solidly for two days and nights, with hardly a movement. As for the elands, they had had their experience. The hunters could not find the heart to kill them. They were allowed to trot off into the bush and Mac saw them no more.

Hunters' dogs generally came to a violent end. The life was hard enough for a man, let alone for his dogs. If man had many enemies in the bush, then the wilderness was crowded with so many dangers for dogs that the wonder was they lived so long at all.

Bvekenya had a second dog: a black, medium-sized animal of uncertain origin. This dog was named Brits and, in his way, he was a curiously cunning animal. He had one special technique of getting rid of fleas, which all dogs adopt in a way, although he was a real expert. He would search out some foul-smelling and noisome piece of filth and roll in it. He would then shake himself vigorously. The fleas, half stunned by the smell, would either jump or be shaken off. Brits would then rush away from the place, and no manner of coaxing would get him back, for fear that the fleas would jump on again.

Brits' end was somewhat unusual. Bvekenya had shot two hippos one day, and the Shanganes had a busy time cutting the skins into sjamboks. They were camped beside some shallow pools in the rock, about two miles from the river. They used one of the pools to soak the sjamboks, and that night the crocodiles in the river got the scent.

The crocodiles stole two miles through the bush, from the river to the pool. There they took all the sjamboks, about 200 of them, worth a good £50.

The hunters were infuriated about it all the next morning. They had put in some hard work on those sjamboks, and to lose them to a crowd of insolent crocodiles was irksome.

As it happened, Brits caught a cane-rat that morning. Bvekenya took it from him, cut it up, and flavoured the pieces with strychnine. Then he buried the pieces in the sand where he knew the crocodiles usually lay. If they liked buried treasure this was going to be some find.

Bvekenya went off hunting for the day. During the night he had heard an elephant breaking trees down in the neighbourhood; and he actually found the animal's trail, where it had drunk at the same pool as he had buried the cane-rat.

Bvekenya followed the trail for a few miles into mupani country. At the edge of a small, boggy stream, he found the elephant. It was a fair-sized bull, grazing without any sign of alarm. Bvekenya watched him carefully.

The elephant had a prodigious appetite. He was consuming mupani leaves seemingly by the ton. He pushed a tree over casually, and then delicately nibbled the green shoots at the top. A few dry boughs followed, crunched up like matchwood, presumably as dessert.

Then the elephant flapped his ears, shook some dust off his hide and walked off downwind, holding his trunk up and smelling the air cautiously to see if anything was following him.

Nothing was following the elephant. Bvekenya was already there, in front of him. As the elephant went into a little hollow, he shot him clean through the heart. The giant had no time to be surprised. He lurched forward down the slope and collapsed.

Bvekenya waited for him to reach the ground. Instead, the elephant seemed to drop a couple of feet and then clambered half-upright. He remained staring straight at Bvekenya, his big ears flapping in the wind.

Bvekenya was astonished. He was certain that he had hit, and hit where it killed. He fired again. There was a thud as the bullet connected, but the elephant budged not an inch.

"Blast all bullet-makers," muttered Bvekenya. "These must be duds."

He fired again, and the gun misfired. The elephant was still staring at him. He dodged behind a tree and opened the gun. The cartridge was loose in the breech and the powder was leaking. He pressed the bullet out hastily, cleaned the gun and reloaded.

The elephant was still in the same position. Once again Bvekenya fired. The gun went off all right, but the elephant didn't flick an eyelid.

"I'll be blowed," said Bvekenya in exasperation. "Either I'm getting a worse shot instead of a better one, or these bullets were all made by someone trying to coin money quicker than a crooked lawyer."

He fired eight shots altogether at that elephant, and it still stood staring at him. It was unbelievable, but the animal was there before him, its ears still flapping and an occasional tremor passing through its body. He walked up to it cautiously, feeling every step, ready to jump the moment the elephant moved.

The elephant was as dead as a spent bullet. In falling, after the first shot, he had collapsed spreadeagled on top of a giant ant heap standing in the hollow. The ant heap had kept the dead animal upright, and its tusks around the top were keeping the body on an even keel. The wind and nervous reactions were moving the ears. The shadows of the branches swaying in the wind gave an illusion of slight tremors in the body. It was a nice bull, with tusks around sixty pounds each. Bvekenya went back to camp to collect his Shanganes. On the way, he turned aside and went down to the pool. It looked as though some woman had been doing washing. There were patches of white scattered all over the place. The crocodiles had found the buried treasure all right. Over eight of them were out for the count, all lying on their backs with their white bellies in the air as token of defeat.

Unfortunately, Brits had also hankered after his cane-rat. He had found his way down to the pool, and there lay his body, among the dead crocodiles, drawn up in the last agony of death from strychnine. Bvekenya buried him in a grave on the banks; but the crocodiles were left lying where they died. That night their cannibal fellows came and ate them; and, as strychnine is remarkably persistent, nearly every crocodile was wiped out in that stretch of river.

Mac, in his time, also came to an equally sudden, if somewhat more glorious end than his former companion. Once, in the camp on the Tshefu, they were lolling around, thinking of moving on to another hunt. In the stillness towards evening, when the pools of the river were afire with the red of the sky, they heard *Khumba*, the bushpig, leading his sows down to the water to drink.

Mac was away with his usual speed. The Shanganes ran after him gleefully, for Khumba is tasty to eat, and a change from a diet of venison was always welcome.

The pigs heard them coming and there was a scurry for the bush. Mac tore after them. As it happened he followed the boar, and the wily old pig led him into the depths of a thicket. There, with the dog entangled in creepers and thorns, the boar turned at bay. He ripped into Mac with a grunt of rage. The dog had no chance in the depths of the bush. Before the Shanganes could frighten the boar off with their noisy approach he had worked his will with his tusks.

They carried Mack back to the camp on the Tshefu. He died in Bvekenya's arms, still grinning and wagging his tail as his master gave him a last pat. They buried him there, in the shade of the trees; and often, long afterwards, in the cool of the evenings while they lazed in their camp, the Shanganes swore they heard from afar the faint clang of a bell and the sound of his bark.

ELEVEN
Mgwazi

T he wilderness in which Bvekenya hunted, between the Great Save and the Limpopo, from the Rhodesian border down to within fifty miles of the sea, was known to the Shanganes as the *Hlengwe* (the place where you need help). It was a place where terror dwelt: a haunt of the wild animals, of sudden death, of an ancient savagery, and the nameless ghosts of strange gods whose lore and rites were half forgotten.

The tribespeople who lived in this desert of bush and sand and swamp were a wild, poverty-stricken and unruly lot. They were sparsely scattered in the bush. The animals, fever, drought, hunger and their own passions kept their numbers down. Foul murders and dreadful barbarities marred the passing of their days, while the spectre of witch-craft haunted their thoughts like a continuous and horrible nightmare.

Their chiefs, for the most part, were a drunken crowd of sots, their brains pickled in spirits, brutal by nature and wholesale debauchers of women. Diviners, witchdoctors and herbalists flourished in every squalid village. The struggle for existence obsessed the people night and day. A man was murdered for the sake of half a sackful of meal, or a woman was corrupted for a handful of sugar. There were few pleasures save drink; and no appreciation, thought, or contact with the outside world save through some dingy store which sold them rum, or cloth, or beads, or stupid little trinkets. The Hlengwe, in short, was not an environment likely at any time to nurture a culture or mother some glorious civilisation.

And yet, in this harsh wild, Bvekenya met several individuals who were peculiarly fascinating characters, and full of the wisdom, the guile, and the ancient legends of their land.

When Bvekenya first went into the bush he met one old, withered character living in a kraal on the Mahonje stream, close to the Tshefu. This individual was a relic of the past, a human museum piece in his way, for he was a proper Knobnose, and one of the last of his kind.

The Knobnoses were a type of African people who were hideously unique. They sported a particular disfigurement, consisting of a variety of giant wart about one and a half inches high, on the tips of their noses.

This wart was artificially induced. It was made by cutting a small strip of skin from the forehead, with a tuft of hair still growing on the end. The strip of skin was peeled down from the forehead and grafted onto the tip of the nose. Once it had taken root in its new home, the skin was disconnected entirely from its former position.

It would then grow on the nose, with the tuft of hair sending long, creeper-like strands out, as the final touch to a hideous disfigurement. Bvekenya questioned the old man about this long obsolete custom, and the story he told as explanation was an almost classic example of African reasoning.

In past years, said the old man, his people were much plagued by the slave raiders. Both Portuguese and Arabs raided them, and life was hardly worth living. No matter how they hid, or where they went, the slavers found them;

and if they fought in order to resist capture, then the best they could expect was a bullet.

Now it so happened that the slavers once raided a certain village. Among the residents of this unfortunate place was a young man who had recently been mauled by a leopard. The leopard had clawed him in the face. Half his forehead had been ripped off, and the loose skin hanging down had accidentally taken root in the form of a revolting lump upon his nose.

The slavers rounded up the inhabitants of the village and examined them. All the good-looking young people who were healthy and able to work were summarily enslaved. The old people were turned loose again as useless, and the disfigured youth was thrown out as being far too hideous.

The tribespeople discussed this event for months. It seemed to them that *Sekwembu*, the great spirit of Providence, had come to aid them. He had sent the leopard to mark them with a special sign. Anybody so marked would escape the slavers.

Thenceforth, then, all young boys and girls were deliberately disfigured by grafting skin from their foreheads to their noses. It was never considered a decoration, affirmed the old man; but better be ugly and free, than handsome and a slave. As they had reasoned, the raiders thenceforth used them only as carriers and never tried to enslave them, for their grotesque appearance destroyed their value in the markets. For generations they continued the disfigurement as their only negative form of defence.

The tribespeople of the Hlengwe were not martial by nature. They made life miserable for one another by an endless series of vicious raids; but these were small-scale affairs, designed to capture women or food supplies. They were brutal, merciless little fights, soon over but never forgotten. Each village nursed bitter hatreds and schemes of vengeance for some ancient wrong. The villages were hidden deep in the bush; and so secret were some of the hideaways that the inhabitants went to great pains to prevent tell-tale paths being made which might lead any unwelcome visitors to their homes.

The tribespeople kept no livestock of their own except an occasional scraggy goat. They lived by hunting, collecting wild fruits, and the produce of a few gardens, carefully hidden in the bush and laboriously tilled with the hard root of the ebony tree for a hoe.

In old age, when hunting had become too strenuous, the Shanganes occasionally resorted to an ingenious scheme to satisfy their hunger for meat. Bvekenya first learned of this scheme in 1916 when he happened to be hunting in the territory of the old headman, Mawasa, son of Masuyamela, the first Shangane leader to settle in the Hlengwe many years ago.

Bvekenya visited Mawasa to pay his respects, and the chief asked him an especial favour.

"Bvekenya, please do not shoot my lion. I always take my share from its kills. It lives near here, in a certain place on the Lundi River which I shall show you."

The request intrigued Bvekenya.

"No, Mawasa, I won't kill your lion. In any case there is nothing I can do with lion skins, but tell me, what is this story about you sharing its kills?"

The old man seemed diffident.

"Others will tell you of that," he said.

Bvekenya duly enquired about Mawasa and his lion. It was quite a story. Every morning the old man would take his bow and arrows and go out to see if the lion had made a kill. The lion was a creature of conservative habits. It hunted at certain water-holes, and was never far from home. Mawasa could always find the kill from the flight of the vultures. He would hobble along eagerly while his wizened-up wife,

Mamukomi, would amble along behind him, carrying a large tin can, a calabash of drinking water, and a bush knife.

At the kill the old man would drive the lion off by shouting and beating a tree trunk with his bow. Then he would cut up the carcass, take what he considered to be the chief's share, give it to his wife to carry home in her tin can, and then leave the remains for the lion, who in a great rage had meanwhile watched proceedings from a suitable vantage point.

On one memorable occasion the lion killed a fine sable bull on the banks of the Lundi, and, hoping to conceal it from Mawasa, laboriously dragged the carcass up a narrow, steep-sided donga. This exhausting work done, the lion returned to the river to drink. At this stage in the proceedings Mawasa arrived and went up the donga, hot on the trail of the kill. The lion must have heard the old man's approach. With an agonised howl it ran into the donga after Mawasa. No sooner had the lion run into the donga than Mamukomi arrived and followed the trail of the other two.

An interesting situation had now developed. Ahead was Mawasa, in the middle was the lion, in the rear was Mamukomi. The old woman saw the lion first. Not realising the true circumstances she commenced beating on her tin can with her bush knife. The lion had heard this before. He ran forward straight at Mawasa. The old man was infuriated. There was his wife callously driving the lion towards him.

"Mamukomi!" he shouted. "I walked to Kimberley in my young days. My brother and friend died of cold and hunger. I worked to get cloth and blankets with which to lobolo you, and now you drive the lion to eat me."

He was dancing and shouting with excitement. The lion paused perplexed. The old woman realised the position. She slowly retreated, calling and beating her tin while the lion followed her. When she reached the mouth of the donga

Mamukomi scrambled up the side, walked hastily along the top to a point above her husband and there passed a pole down to help the old man to safety. He carried the meat with him, and all Bvekenya could say when they showed him the donga with its dead end and steep 15-feet walls, was – "It must be a very well-behaved lion!"

The Shanganes had few crafts or industries. Some cotton was spun from the wild cotton bushes, and they carved headrests from the soft wood of the marula trees. Iron was also beaten skilfully enough into spearheads. In former years the base metal was obtained from distant mines in the Transvaal. In recent times, however, the migrant labourers always brought back old files or pieces of crowbars when they returned home; and these were used to manufacture spears.

It was in hunting that the Shanganes of the Hlengwe really excelled. Hunting was their proudest occupation. Every village boasted some expert hunter who specialised in the task of providing meat for his fellows, while the others acted as his assistants and resorted to the most ingenious schemes to obtain ammunition for their champion.

They used bows and arrows, dug pits, and had a genius for making traps and snares. They would even attack an elephant with bows and arrows. It was no uncommon thing for an expert bowman to kill an elephant with one arrow straight in the heart, while even an inferior shot would sooner or later prove fatal, for all their weapons were poisoned.

Guns were particularly prized by them, and they would give anything to possess a good rifle. They went to the length of making crude guns of their own out of unrifled pipes, which fired pebbles, hard marula pips, and a variety of other objects: lethal if they hit the target, more lethal if they exploded in the hunter's face.

Ammunition was always scarce. Every returning migrant worker would try to smuggle home a supply of powder, filched from the mines by means of furtively unravelling fuses somewhere in the dark, thousands of feet down a shaft.

They would secrete this powder about their persons: in the hair, concealed in their clothing, or hidden in hollowed-out cakes of soap. One man managed to fill up a whole calabash with gunpowder. It was a treasure, enough to buy him several wives. He had a second calabash full of water to sustain him on the journey.

As he tramped along the Rhodesian border he encountered a police patrol, searching the mine labourers for gunpowder. They stopped him, along with his companions. He sat down miserably, waiting to be searched, while his companions were each forced to give up their small secretions of powder.

The policemen were perspiring in the heat.

"Have some water, masters?" asked the man, with a touch of genius.

The policemen accepted readily. He gave them his calabash of water. They drained it. With his heart in his mouth, he offered the second calabash.

"No," said one of the policemen kindly. "Keep that for yourself, you'll need it on this path."

They searched him and found nothing on his person. He picked up his precious calabash and went on along the path. It was a thirsty journey home, but he sang all the way.

Bullets and powder were always so scarce that a Shangane hunter would nurse his supply to incredible limits. He would wait for days to shoot an antelope, lying in ambush until the animal eventually came so near that it was next to impossible to miss and the hunter could use the barest minimum of powder. If he did miss he would spend a day or more beating the bush, raking the ground to recover the bullet, and then hammer it back into shape and use it all over again.

The needs of the Shanganes were few, and in a normal season the bush supplied all their wants. It was as though Providence realised the drab hardship of life in the wilds and was thoughtful enough to provide some entertainment besides the bare necessities of life. Scattered throughout the bush were immense numbers of lala palms (*Hyphaene crinita*). These palms not only yield their leaves for thatching and mat-making, but their nuts are the favourites of both man and the baboons; and their sap provides in generous quantity what is without doubt the world's greatest free liquor supply.

In settled areas, every lala palm is the property of some individual, and any wilful damage done to it is sure to arouse protest. The palms are carefully watched until they reach maturity. Then, during the dry months, they are trimmed down to the stumps, a groove cut around, about two inches from the top, and a leaf inserted which acts as a sort of spout. Below this spout a calabash is suspended, to catch the sap forced out of the trunk in a steady drip for about five weeks. Every day a fresh, paper-thin slice is cut off the trunk, in order to prevent any sealing tissue from forming.

This sap of the lala palm makes a pleasant drink when fresh: when fermented it has a kick like a giraffe. Given a good number of palm trees around him, a Shangane could (and many did) stay drunk from infancy to old age; and thus have the distinction of being buried sozzled after the unique experience of having been very nearly born that way.

The elephants (especially old bulls) also had a liking for this potent lala palm wine. They could not make it themselves, but at least they could steal it from the

Shanganes. In the season, they would go from palm tree to palm tree and skilfully empty each calabash with their trunks. As they travelled, they became noisier. Towards the end they made a terrific uproar. At night, particularly, the noise would sometimes be tremendous. One would think a whole herd of elephants was trumpeting, instead of just one very tipsy animal.

A supply of palm wine, or the equally potent marula beer, and some venison, were enough to provide the ingredients for a celebration. The occasion would be the coming of age of their girls or youths, a wedding or just some minor excuse to make merry and work up to a murder or a free fight.

Whatever it was, the Shanganes would order a drummer up some tall tree to send a message over the bush. Often in the early mornings, when the air was calm and clear, Bvekenya would hear the drumming from miles away.

"Du, du, dum-dum," would go the drum, over and over again, inviting the people to a feast, or informing the local world in general that Bvekenya had arrived and there was an elephant to eat. But again, the drum might say with warning in its voice: "Dum, dum, du-du, dum, dum, du-du," to tell its listeners that trouble was near or that the police-boys who ruled the bush were travelling the paths with sjamboks in their hands.

The lala palms yielded their sap several times during the year, but the season of the marula or *Mkanye* berries was so important that several months in the year were named in honour of the fruit.

The Shangane calendar, in fact, is at all times related closely to the crops and the condition of the wild animals and fruits.

January is the month when the marula fruit is ripe, and all the people of the wilderness joyously embark on a full-time carousal. *Hoho* is the apt Shangane name for this month – a month of laughter and festivity.

February is the month of *Mhlanga*, when the young grain (as the name implies) is showing like reeds, tall and green and waving in the winds.

March is the month of *Jubamsoko*. It is the month when the rains (if they have come at all) have turned the wilderness into a green jungle, with the trees and creepers densely clothed in leaves and the pathways all so overgrown with grass that, as the name implies, it has to be "cut down" to allow the passage of man.

April is the pleasant month of *Mkwekwezi*, when man can first "eat of the crops."

May is the busy month of *Sandwela*, the time of "reaping", when the people are all out in the fields gathering in the rewards of months of hard work, and ceaseless warfare against the creatures of the wilds who have sought throughout the summer months to raid their growing crops.

June is *Sheremela*, the month of "hoeing", when the whole annual programme of agriculture is started again with the first backbreaking chores of the women.

July is the month of *Konyane*, when the maize cobs in the storage huts are "ripe and dry" and golden.

August sees the first hope of spring breathe its magic life into the sleeping wilderness. It is the month of *Komkulu*, the month when the trees are just beginning to bud.

September is the month of keen anticipation, for it is the month of *Sekanwane*, when the marula trees show their flowers and the Shanganes feel the first pangs of their coming thirst.

October is the month of *Kanamkulu*, when the marula fruits are big and man can judge the coming harvest in terms of gallons of beer.

November is the month of *iMpala*, when the mpala antelopes drop their young, and the bush seems alive with the perky little fawns and their anxious mothers.

December is the month of *Nkokoni*, for it is then that

Nkokoni, the blue wildebeest, gives birth to its young; and the Shanganes know by this event that the year is over. Through all its dangers and troubles they have passed in safety; and only one more moon must move through its relentless changes and all the merriness of *Hoho* will be with them once again.

One unusual activity carried on in the Hlengwe all through the year was the collection of articles for the bizarre pharmacopoeia of witchdoctors. Mozambique has always been a great manufactory of herbs and medicines for the African witchdoctor, while enormous quantities of animal skins have been exported through the years to supply the demand, especially in Zululand and the Witwatersrand, for the fancy costumes used for dancing. At some seasons of the year, particularly in April, it was traditional for practically the entire male population to turn out and trap the little spotted and striped *Simba* (genet) which was active then and possessed a coat highly regarded by the dancers of Africa.

It was through this ancient traffic in medicines and skins that Bvekenya met Mgwazi. During the time of the drought, he was once camped near the Great Save River. The local chief, Mafunjwa, came to him one day and asked a favour.

Mafunjwa was a good friend of Bvekenya's, and as such he was inclined to help the man if there was anything reasonable which he could do. Mafunjwa told him that he had an old herbalist staying in his village. He was a renowned character in the trade, who came around to those parts once every six or seven years to obtain items for his magic practice. He wandered from the Kalahari to Mozambique; to the Sotho country; to Zululand; and to Rhodesia. In each area he traded the medicines and talismans needed by his kind, and had a vast store of knowledge, observation, mysticism and African lore, picked up in the course of his travels.

The name of this wanderer was Mgwazi. He had come to the Hlengwe in search of *Ndlandlama*, the black Samango monkey. There the drought and famine had caught him and made it difficult to travel, for he was old, incapable of hunting for himself; and, although he was popular with the local tribespeople, they were so hard pressed themselves that they found it difficult to provide the food to support him.

The favour Mafunjwa asked was that Bvekenya allow the old magician to attach himself to the hunting party as a camp follower, living on their bounty and such meat as they could spare until the rains came.

Bvekenya was quite agreeable. His camp had few comforts. At that time it hardly weighed more than twenty pounds when packed. It consisted of one grease-can, a beaker, a frying pan, a piece of canvas sail, a mosquito net and one blanket. Anyone attaching himself to such a camp could hardly expect much; but at least there was generally an ample supply of meat.

Old Mgwazi, therefore, came over and introduced himself. He was a tall, scraggy-looking character, with a reddish beard. He looked about eighty years of age. His whole person was festooned with little calabashes hanging on thongs, while sundry baskets and sacks containing his supplies of medicines were slung over his shoulder.

Bvekenya was following elephants at the time; but the animals were uncommonly wary and he never caught them. Instead, he found two hippos foolishly trying to hide in a pool much too shallow for them; and he shot one to provide some food.

Oddly enough, while his own Shanganes and the tribespeople were jubilant at the kill, he noticed that the old herbalist seemed annoyed.

He saw Bvekenya looking at him, and said in a disgruntled

voice: "It is because you white men shoot these hippos that we have such droughts in my own country."

Bvekenya was somewhat ruffled at the criticism.

"Eat, and be thankful," he snapped.

The hippo was cut up and soon disposed of, skin and all. The bones were too tough. Bvekenya noticed that the herbalist was not remiss in eating the animal.

When the feast was over and they were all pleasantly full and resting in the shade of the trees, he called the herbalist over.

"Mgwazi," he asked, "what is the matter with you? You are against us shooting *Mpfuvu*, the hippo, and yet you are happy enough to eat him. What is your complaint?"

The old man arranged his calabashes and settled himself down with his back to a tree.

"Chief," he said, "I am a Zulu."

Bvekenya nodded. He had long noticed the man's aloofness and slight air of condescension to the Shanganes.

"So," he said. "I had suspected that you were of Shaka's people. Now tell me, what is this about white men and hippos?"

"Chief," said Mgwazi, "to understand this matter you must first understand how it is that I, a Zulu, now have my home in the desert in the west: that place which the Tswana people call the *Kgaligadi* (Kalahari). My father ran away from his chief. Shaka was dead and Dingane was the lord of the Zulus, and many people had been killed by that murderer of his own brother.

"My father was henchman to Mdlaka, marshal of the army. When Dingane killed Shaka he also twisted the neck of Mdlaka, for he well knew that the officers of the army were all firm for Shaka.

"My father fled with his people. For four seasons he wandered westwards, across the high plains, until he reached the desert and found a hiding place at the great water known as Ngami.

"Near this place, on the banks of the Okavango River, my father settled with his people: only a handful of Zulus living alone in that far land. There they lived peacefully through the years. There I was born, and one winter, when I was just starting to herd my father's cattle, the first white men came: certain buyers and sellers of goods, who brought with them wagons and oxen and *izibamu* (guns).

"These white men traded *izibamu* for cattle, ivory, skins and ostrich feathers: all of which we then possessed and, indeed, traded with brown people who came from the east.

"Now, you must know that in those times the Okavango was indeed a mighty river and Ngami was a sheet of water like unto the sea. There were hippos in all the waterways in numbers beyond count, and they gave us much trouble in the lands.

"When the corn was ripening we had to beat drums all night to drive the hippos away, while the women spent all day frightening the birds off. Between the birds and the hippos, the people had no rest until the crops were reaped and safely stored away.

"Now these hippos were cunning. We dug deep pits to catch them, but seldom did they ever fall in. Then the white men came with their guns which could kill hippos. They shot one of them, to show us how easy it was with their weapons; and to make us anxious to possess these wonderful things, no matter how high the price.

"So our people bought all the guns for which they had cattle or ivory or goods; and each gun was only bought if the white men proved it by shooting one hippo.

"Then, when spring came, the white men went off with their wagons full of our things, driving our cattle before them, and leaving us with the guns.

"Now life was very good. The white men had shown us

how to make sledges and break in oxen with neck-yokes, so that the women no longer had to carry everything.

"We shot the hippos and we killed much game. Our crops were good and even the dogs were sleek and fat from feasting on the venison.

"But then we noticed that each year the reeds in the river channels were growing bigger and bigger. Soon they covered the river altogether; and when the floods came, vast masses of reeds were washed down, like floating islands, and these blocked up all the narrow passages. You see, there were no longer any hippos to eat the reeds, or to force new passages through them.

"Then, one morning after the rains had started, the women went to fetch water. They came running back, calling the men to come and see the river. It was in flood, and in its waters there came down countless numbers of floating reed islands.

"Where the water entered Ngami the reeds jammed up into a solid barrier, and season after season this barrier choked up tighter and tighter. The barrier of reeds was like a wall. We were driven from our lands when the water was pushed back and flooded beyond its ancient banks.

"So it lasted for many seasons. Then, far away, the weight of the waters forced a new passage for the river and it flowed in a new direction.

"We tried to destroy the barrier of reeds by firing it, but we could not succeed. The river flowed elsewhere. Each year the country changed. It became drier and drier. Droughts came upon us, where before there was plenty. The desert crept into our gardens and stole our crops, and there were no drums we could beat to drive it away.

"Instead of the misty rains we had enjoyed of old, there now came only sandstorms and thirst. The land became a wilderness, with dead stumps instead of green forests; and Ngami, instead of a sea, became a bowl of dust. All this was because you white men taught us the mystery of guns and how to kill the hippos, who for all the forgotten years had kept the rivers open; and although we did not know it and hunted them as thieves, were more truly our friends than those accursed guns which have brought more sadness to this world than good. May those who first made them be despised by all the spirits."

Bvekenya listened to him in silence.

"You have spoken well Mgwazi," he said. "Your knowledge is deep and your wisdom as great as your age. You are also a teller of fine and wonderful things. In the evenings, at our camps, you must henceforth sleep closer to the fire and have more meat. In payment for this, you shall tell us stories and speak of those strange things which you have heard and seen. Now let us sleep. Tomorrow is for work, and the days are longer than the nights."

Somebody threw fresh logs upon the fire, and the camp dozed off. There was no sound save the wind in the trees and the call of some bird who had lost its mate in the emptiness of the sky.

TWELVE
Mgwazi's story

For nearly two years Mgwazi remained with Bvekenya. He feasted when the hunters had venison, and made no complaint if the guns were silent and there was hunger. He was no trouble, but rather an endless source of entertainment, for his stories were always lively and well told.

Bvekenya had shot an eland one day, and the whole camp was delighted. *Mhofu* (the eland) was always popular with the hunters. Of all antelope his meat is the most tender (full of flavour and with just the right amount of fat) and they feasted well that night.

When they were finished they settled back and looked expectantly at Mgwazi. They had few other entertainments or pleasures, but he never failed them. Bvekenya sometimes longed for tobacco (he had never descended to the lengths of a few others and resorted to elephant droppings); but he always found the stories of Mgwazi a fine after-dinner substitute for the drinks, conversation and smokes of conventional society.

Mgwazi cleared his throat and began.

"Chiefs," he said, "at this time of drought and hunger it is fitting that we should speak of Mujaji, the Queen of the Rain, and her tribe of the Lobedu. Truly, it must be because the people no longer send her what is her due that the rains are gone and the land is parched. She is the transformer of the clouds, the maker of the rain, the bringer of drought, locusts or pestilence; and it is because you white men, and all those black people who have forgotten the ways of their fathers, now treat her with scorn, that there is hunger in the land.

"Listen to me. I tell you truly that in past years this Mujaji was the queen of all wizards. She was the one who was, and yet was not. No man saw her, she was invisible; and yet, like the winds, she could still be felt and her voice be heard; and her will was law; and her desires were to be implicitly obeyed. Her likeness no man knows for sure; and yet she lives forever in a secret grove, as far away and distant, and yet seeing all things, as an eagle in its eyrie."

Bvekenya grunted.

"I have heard of this woman before. She lives in the mountains of the Eastern Transvaal. Among my own people there are men who have spoken and written much about this *She who must be obeyed*. What is the truth of the matter?"

"Chief," said Mgwazi, "I have heard many strange tales of this woman and the secret of her magic. Listen to me. I tell you that in the beginning, when my ancestors were still in the north, in that land where lie the lakes beside which Nguni, the founder of our kind, was born, there lived in Bokhalaka (Rhodesia) the Kalanga people, whose chief was a mighty lord, with armies and many followers skilled in mining and in building great villages of stone.

"It happened that this lord had a daughter called Mujaji, one who was desirable beyond words. She was both wise and beautiful; and in her wisdom she well knew of the trouble which her beauty could bring. Men contended for her hand in marriage. There were suitors who came from afar, bringing many presents with which to woo her favours. All such things were pleasant, for she was above all things a woman, with the vanity of her kind, and the rivalry of young men in love is always pleasant.

"But where her trouble came was this. Her own brother, he who was the heir and favourite of the chief, desired her. This was an evil, and she was afraid. While her father lived, the brother would do little save suppress his evil passions; but should her father die, she was well aware that her brother would seize her and work his will, for he would be the lord whom all must obey: the maker of his own decrees, the satisfier of his own whims and passions.

"Now it happened that her father grew sick: whether of age, or owing to the devices of his son who was impatient for his inheritance, I know not. But the princess, his sister, well knew that as her father breathed his last there approached a fate more hideous than any demon in her dreams.

"So she spoke with her people, those who were her especial followers and friends; and they resolved to steal away, taking with them only such goods as they could carry, and find some new home for themselves, some fertile and peaceful spot in the wilderness where they would be beyond the reach of the evil brother.

"The princess arranged that she went to pray at the ancestral graves for the spirit of her father; and from those secret places she stole away to meet her people and flee beyond the waters of the Limpopo in the south, before the young chief, in his new vanity and glory, could suspect the wrong.

"The Kalanga lord was much enraged when he found his sister gone. His desire was turned to hate. He sent his men southwards through the bush, travelling fast, with spears in their hands and death in their thoughts; but a weary chase did the princess lead them.

"Only one of all the pursuing bands ever caught up with the refugees. That one band might have been enough, for it was powerful and the refugees were weak; but the princess was wise. The spirits were also kind. The pursuers came towards their victims in the thick, dry, winter bush. The wind was blowing in their faces, and the princess caused the grass to be fired so that the flames might form a barrier of burning bush.

"The fire was more successful than she had hoped. It burned the bush, and not a few of her pursuers; and in the smoke and confusion she led her people into the night, and the lands of Bokhalaka knew them no more.

"The search for some new home, where she could live in peace, took the princess far south from her former land. She searched in every direction, sending young men to spy out the country and discover the nature of its people.

"Many wonders did these spies discover, and strange were the reports they returned. Among them was one young warrior whose name was Thana: a handsome man, and brave in heart. He it was, devoted to his princess's command, who travelled farthest and in the end brought back a spray of green leaves, with wild fruits pleasant to the taste, and wild flowers that were delightful to the eye.

"'Whence come these?' asked the princess in surprise.

"'My lady,' answered Thana, 'there is a certain forest which I have found. It is not big and yet not too small. It lies in a valley which is but a segment of a larger valley. It is a place of great trees, of greenness, of clear water and wild fruits. There the antelope play and the birds are so tame that it is certain no man disturbs the tranquillity of their home. And besides all this, there is a marvel there. I found the entrance to a cavern, vast and black and reaching to the mysteries of the earth. I had no light, I could not probe its depths, but I am certain that all our people and ten thousand more could find a hiding place in the safety of its shadows.'

"To this place, then, Mujaji led her people, with Thana as her guide; and, indeed, it was all the young man had said. Still, today, this forest of Daja is a green and mysterious place; but of its inner secrets I can tell you nothing, for it is taboo, and no stranger enters there and lives.

"In this forest the princess and her people built a village and made their gardens. The soil was good, the rain was plentiful, and the people prospered and were content. Yet their princess had many worries. She well knew that this forest sanctuary was secure only so long as it was remote from others.

"Should her people increase, or news of their prosperity be spread abroad, then jealous persons would come quickly to steal their goods and spoil their lives.

"So she pondered much upon the future, and with her elders debated often on what should best be done for the security and happiness of her people.

"Now, her favourite councillor was a certain greybeard named Matala. This Matala was aged, and wise in the legends of his people. In past times, in Bokhalaka, he had been a priest and doctor, skilled in the rituals of the nation – the magic with which they made the rain, and the divining of the future – a medium closely acquainted with the spirits.

"'My lady,' this Matala said to his princess one day, 'it seems to me that this perplexity about the future which plagues us may easily be banished.'

"'How so?' enquired the princess.

"'My lady,' said Matala, 'it is needful that we ask the favour and guidance of the spirits.'

"'And how may this be done?'

"'There is no obstacle greater than our own doubt. In past times, as my lady knows, I was the priest and doctor to our king. Think you that I have forgotten my former skills? Or that I neglected to bring from Bokhalaka certain medicines and magics needful in communing with the spirits? Besides, your own self, in the manner of the royal house of our people, you have certain knowledge and training as a priestess of our faith.'

"'That is so, but I have half forgotten it. It was my brother's duty to serve the spirits and make the rain. I was

145

shown when I was little, but took small notice, for it was never meant to be the task of women.'

"'I will remind you of those things you have forgotten. It is your privilege, because of your blood, to have communion at least once with your ancestors. They will advise us. Now, listen closely and I will tell you how this magic works.'

"For the phases of one moon Matala taught his princess what he knew; and in the end she was ready, although full of doubts. For their magic, they decided upon an inner corner of the cave: a place where none could disturb or watch or overhear them; and it was to this place that Matala and Mujaji made their way when all things were prepared.

"There was no pleasure in the darkness of that cave. The bats and other evil things had their dwellings there; and there were many strange sounds and echoes, and white pillars that came from the roof to meet companions from the floor.

"In an open place, a sort of inner chamber in that mighty cavern, Mujaji and Matala set themselves to make their magic. Mujaji had learned her lessons well. There was no speech between them, only the noise of water dripping in the distance and the flurry of strange wings beating the air.

"Mujaji worked her magic and so caused a tiny flame to come to life in the cave before her. She fed it with her spells, until of a sudden it exploded into fire of many colours and surprising fierceness, but with no heat.

"And then, within the strange movements of the flames, there came a face: a sort of demon to the eye, and yet by nature neither good nor bad.

"'Mujaji, Mujaji, Mujaji,' whispered the face, with a voice like the sound of the flames burning, though the fire itself was still. 'You summon us for this one meeting from our ancestral places in the lost worlds. What would you have?'

"Mujaji was stricken silent by her fear.

"The fire spirit laughed at her, with soft and curious noises.

"'Why so afraid, Mujaji? You brought me here. Now would you have me gone? How like a woman! But no matter. I know more of you than you do yourself. You have a question to ask. It is already answered. These tribes around you that you fear so much are as barbarous as they are fierce. You cannot conquer them, nor hold your own by force of arms. Therefore, place your trust in guile and cunning. In this wild, great store is set upon the rain: it is a precious thing. Trade upon the skill of your forefathers. Ever were they masters of the magic of the rain. Weave your spells. The tribes will pay you much for rain, while for fear of being cursed with drought they will grant you all respect.'

"'But I have not the medicines to make rain,' said Mujaji in wonder.

"'That is no great obstacle. The medicines are four in number. Obtain them, and Matala will teach you their use.'

"'What are they?'

"'There is the medicine of strength and fertility. The Venda in the mountains to your north have such a medicine: go and obtain it. There is the medicine of cunning and wisdom. It is really two medicines, for cunning and wisdom do not often mix. This medicine is with the Ndebele people who live to your west. Seek it!

"'Then there is the medicine of magic and transformation. It is a magic well known to your own people. In the old places of your fathers, where the lizards and the lions still live, the medicine may be found.'

"'And the fourth medicine?'

"'That is the medicine of your own power. That we and the love of your own people alone can give you.'

"'Will you give it?'

"'For a price, yes. The price of the sacrifice of one who is your own, whose life must be given us willingly by himself and who will be your champion in the skies.'

"'How can I ask that of anyone?' said Mujaji in unhappiness. But the fire spirit laughed with fading sounds.

"'It is ordained, Mujaji, it is ordained. We will take that which is our due for our help. Now do as I have told, and have no fear. Your champion will vanquish even death itself for you.'

"The fire died and the spirit vanished, and Mujaji and Matala left the cave.

"For long, Mujaji and Matala discussed the message of the fire spirit. Mujaji was half inclined to think that all she had seen and heard was just illusion, but Matala had no doubts. They must immediately despatch young men to secure the medicines; and of all those present there was none more confident or bold than Thana.

"So the young man was summoned before his lady and told of her needs. He had no doubts about his prowess.

"'The reward will be yours to command,' she promised him; and he smiled, for he had certain ideas which involved more than servitude to Mujaji. So he left, while she saw him off, hoping truly that he would soon be back, even if he failed to bring the medicines.

"Now, Thana travelled many miles through the forest and the bush to reach the mountains where dwelt the Venda people. Strange animals, and birds coloured like the rainbow did he see upon that journey; and many adventures did he have. And in the end he found upon the horizon the range of mountains, lying there in purple colour, very tall and far away.

"He made his way towards these mountains and found a path which led him to the heights, where the clouds made marriage with the peaks and produced merry streamlets as their offspring.

"In those heights he found the Venda villages, and

thought it strange to find them all deserted save for dogs and fowls. He went onwards to other huts and villages and found them also empty, although the embers in the fireplaces were still warm and much beer was in the pots.

"Then, while he stood and puzzled on these deserted villages, he heard the sound of distant drums. He went towards this sound, thinking at first that he might have confused drums with thunder; but on the pathway which he followed were the tracks of many feet. The path took him nearer and nearer to the sound of the drums, until in the end he reached a summit, and there below him was a lake.

"Now this lake was enchanted. Calm lay its waters, in a deep valley set with mountains. Blue seemed its surface, like the sky; and deep below certain spirits are said to live, with villages, and cattle grazing beneath the waters; and the sound of drums is often heard in the night.

"Beside this lake there stood a vast throng of people. Fires burned among them, drums beat; and certain maidens, very young and sleek, with beads all made of silver, did strange dances in the centre.

"Thana stole down upon this throng with care and interest, for he knew not what they did. Strange things did he see. There were witchdoctors and diviners there in great numbers; and a certain figure, made of grass, which spoke in whistles and danced wild dances in the air, with only magic for support.

"Suddenly there was a great commotion in the midst of the entertainment. The doctors had seized one of the dancing maidens. All ran aside, save one, who was the sister of the victim. She tried to aid her sister, but the doctors beat her to the ground. Then they dressed their selected maiden in grass and curious clothes and put medicines on her person. When they were done, they led her to the water. The girl walked in, very frightened, until the water reached her thighs. And then, while Thana watched, there came of a sudden a disturbance in the water; and while the assembled people raised a shout, a mighty serpent, greater by far even than *Hlathu*, the python, came swimming to the surface and threw its coils around the girl.

"This was too much for Thana. He left his hiding place and ran down to help the girl. But the people saw him. Warriors seized him and held him fast, while the serpent wrapped its coils around the screaming maiden and then drew her downwards through the water, out of sight.

"So there was an end to the matter; but not for Thana. All night they held him captive in a hut, while the sound of dancing and singing was heard from outside.

"When morning came they led him outside, with his hands still tied behind him. There was feasting and celebration and the sweet sound of the wooden instruments which the Venda called *timbilas*. They led Thana through the throng until he stood before their chief.

"The chief looked him up and down.

"'Who are you, and from whence?' He asked. 'For what reason did you seek to disturb our ritual?'

"Thana told him of his mission.

"'Sir,' he said, when he had finished, 'knowing now what brought me to your realm, how can you blame me for seeking to save that maiden from so vile a monster? You must be demons to allow so barbarous a custom.'

"'Woh,' said the chief, 'listen to this bold cockerel. Know you that each year we hold these celebrations? That reptile you describe so ill is none other than the God and generous spirit of all our prosperity and rain. Each year he takes one maiden to be his wife. If he accepts the one we offer, then the season will be good. And as for the loss of one single maiden: what can a woman offer, compared to the delights of a full belly? He is welcome to her, if, in exchange, his gift is food. My cockerel, you must be young indeed if you would give a woman preferment to your own stomach.

"'As for this medicine your queen has sent you to fetch

from us, it is the very medicine of fertility and strength which that reptile grants us. You would have it for your own, yet you revile us for our method of obtaining it. Man is always like that. Somebody else must soil his hands, so that others, more upright, may take it from him and be unsullied.

"'As for this medicine you want. I am in the mood for entertainment, for today we celebrate the marriage of our God.'

"He called his councillors to him and sent one off, laughing, on an errand. Presently there came before the chief a warrior of vast stature and strength.

"'See this man,' said the chief to Thana. 'To his belt I tie this pouch. Within the pouch there lies a quantity of the medicine you crave. It is a portion of the skin of that self-same reptile which you abhor. Each year he sloughs off his skin; and folded in the bag is sufficient to last your queen a thousand years and more. Go, take it. We would have sport. Receive your weapons. The prize is yours: but fight for it.' And he laughed.

"There was no choice for Thana. The Venda would certainly cause his death; and now at least he could die fighting. So he took his weapons, which they returned to him; and when the people had seated themselves in a large circle, playing drums and timbilas, he went with their champion to the centre and prepared for battle. Of all the watching throng, none gave him sympathy save one, and she was the sister of the python's bride, whom Thana had sought to aid and who was among the other maidens beating their drums.

"Of the fight there is much that is still remembered. The Venda was a lusty fighter, but Thana was light and agile and very rapid in his blows. For long raged the battle, with spear and club and shield crashing one against the other, and the multitude of people watching silently.

"The Venda fetched Thana a blow with his club, so

stunning that he knocked the young man's shield away. He fought on with just a spear, but his plight was sad. The Venda bore down upon him with shouts of triumph, and beneath this weight Thana was thrown upon the ground, but he still clutched his spear and clung to hope.

"He rolled over on the ground, dodging the blows of his rival and seeking to stab him in the legs. He looked for a chance, and his one friend in that watching throng found it for him. Of a sudden there was a mighty crash. In the silence she had beaten the largest drum, with a blow that was like a thunderclap. The Venda looked around in surprise, and Thana found his chance. Within the instant, he drove his spear deep within the warrior's stomach and then stripped him of his pouch as he rolled howling on the ground.

"Thus the first medicine of Mujaji was found, for the Venda chief held to his word. Thana left them, with many tokens of their esteem. Having taken gallant leave of she who had been his unexpected ally, he once more took the pathway along which he had first journeyed, and made his way southwards to his home."

"And tomorrow we, too, follow a long pathway," interrupted Bvekenya. "Let us sleep now. The light will come sooner than we want it. Early evening is for stories, and there will be many more opportunities for you to complete the tale."

So they made their beds and slept, with only the fire still awake, as the guardian of their lonely camp.

THIRTEEN
African nights

No hunter is lucky all the time. On the Tshefu River Bvekenya once came across the relics of a curious tragedy. Some time before a lion must have hunted an eland bull there and brought the animal to bay. Judging from the signs on the ground there must have been a long and bitter battle, the eland fighting it out with his back to a tree.

In the end the lion sprang and broke the eland's neck. This was the usual end to such a combat; but in this case there was a sequel. The eland fell and jammed its horns through the skin of the lion's neck, pinning him against the tree trunk and suffocating him to death.

Bvekenya never had a misfortune comparable to this, but he had one most unusual run of bad luck. The day after Mgwazi told the first part of his story about the Rain Queen, Bvekenya set out to reach the banks of the Tshefu River. It was a long trek, and there was little game in the miles of bush through which he travelled.

Then, when he reached the upper Tshefu, he shot a zebra. He was in the territory of a petty headman named Mahonoke: a surly character who was busily employed at that time in the irritating business of moving his village to a new site, the usual practice followed by the Shanganes when their old homes became infested with vermin.

Perhaps the removal, or the sleepless nights of insect bites preliminary to it, made Mahonoke more than usually sullen. Whatever the reason, he suddenly demanded that the chief's full portion of an animal (the hindquarters and breast) be awarded him. Bvekenya just sent him a portion of roasted meat, with the message that he was lucky even to get that.

There was no reply from Mahonoke, but presently a rumour came through the bush that the headman, in a great rage, had summoned the neighbouring witchdoctors and bewitched Bvekenya so that he could no longer hunt.

Bvekenya was amused when his hunters told him of the rumour.

"Do you think I am a child, to believe such nonsense?"

They simply stared at him, with a curious sort of blankness.

Time passed. Game seemed scarce, and his aim was atrocious even when he found something. He could not even shoot a monkey to feed the dogs. He was reduced to buying goats from the tribespeople, and this was a sad come-down indeed. Then, one night, Mgwazi came to him.

"Chief," he said, "you white men have your ways, and we have ours. Be still for a while, and let me examine the matter. I hunger, and your hunters also; and these goats you buy are tough, and stink besides."

He settled down and threw the bones: a choice collection of magical objects, ranging from odd foreign coins to curiously coloured pebbles and real bones. There was even one domino among the items. Bvekenya wondered, with some interest, what the individual histories of these various items had been before they reached Mgwazi's hands.

Mgwazi had no doubt of the state of affairs after his reading.

"It is true," he said, "your gun has been closed."

He went off, and for some hours sat trancelike against a tree. The hunters left him alone. He was consulting the

154

ancestral spirits, they told Bvekenya. It was only after some hours that Mgwazi came back to life. He seemed to have dismissed the matter from his thoughts. The hunters were in festive mood.

"Tomorrow we kill again," they told Bvekenya. "The spell is broken."

Bvekenya was sceptical, but he gave the old man a shilling and four feet of calico as a reward for his trouble. The next day, before dawn, his hunters aroused him.

"Sir," they said, "today we eat. Let us be off."

They set about the hunt with such alacrity that even the doubting Bvekenya was intrigued. Two hours from camp they found a kudu cow browsing on the bush. Bvekenya had his 9.5 rifle with him. He sent a shot crashing through the silence of the bush, and there was no doubt that it had hit.

But he had no immediate time to investigate the fallen kudu. No sooner had the shot crashed out than three old buffalo bulls (of the age when they are generally cast out by their herds and called *gwelos* by the Shanganes) started up from a nearby hollow and galloped heavily past him. Bvekenya fired one, two, three quick shots as the animals vanished through the bush.

He was about to start after them when his gun-boy, Kommetje, pulled his arm and pointed. On a rise about 500 yards away he saw an elephant, also startled by the firing, stalking off between two trees. It was a ridiculously long distance, but Bvekenya lifted his gun and fired the longest shot he had ever used in the hope of killing an elephant.

It had certainly been a warm few minutes. He stood listening intently, to hear which way the elephant ran. There was no sound. He walked cautiously up the rise, listening carefully as he went. There was no sign of the elephant. He walked straight to the place where he had last seen the animal.

The bush was dense. Bvekenya pushed his way through it, with one eye on the tracks and the other watching for the elephant. He moved one branch aside, and pushed his face right into the elephant's foot. By some miracle, the long shot had found the elephant's heart. The animal had tumbled over into a small donga and landed on its back. It had died with its feet in the air and was a nice prize, with handy sixty pound tusks. After the weeks of failure Bvekenya was delighted.

He went down the slope to call his hunters. He found them examining the dead kudu cow and making preparations for a fire.

"What happened to the buffalo?" he asked.

They looked at him, startled. They had forgotten those three animals. They soon found their tracks, and soon found them as well. The three bulls were lying dead or dying, only fifty yards away. It seemed impossible. With five shots he had hit five animals, all within two minutes, when before that he had hunted for nearly a month and shot nothing.

It was the sort of thing that he had always derided, when others boasted of similar achievements. Now he was very much in the position of a man who had just seen a ghost after being a sceptic all his life. He had the mortification of knowing that if he had never been prepared to believe anyone else before, now nobody was ever going to believe him.

Back at camp that night, the hunters were almost drugged from over-eating. Mgwazi had been awarded a substantial share of the choicest portions, although Bvekenya could still hardly bring himself to believe in the magic.

"All right," he said to his Shanganes. "If he did do it, what did he do?"

"Sir," they replied, "by his magic he caused Mahonoke to have hiccups."

"To have hiccups?"

"Sir, it is so. He could neither eat nor drink nor sleep nor enjoy his wives. By morning he had called off his curse, for he well knew the origin of his trouble."

"And has Mgwazi cured his hiccups?"

"Sir, he is thinking of it. Maybe tomorrow he will do it; but he is not certain he remembers the cure."

Bvekenya had a respect for witchdoctors ever after that. Good cheer prevailed at the campfire that night. When they had finished eating Bvekenya called Mgwazi over, and the hunters gathered around in anticipation.

"Mgwazi," said Bvekenya, "you may have certain un-finished business; but an unfinished story is not sufferable. There was a matter of the Rain Queen, Mujaji. Let us hear the end of it."

"Chiefs," said Mgwazi, "when Thana returned to his own people with the first medicine they made much of him, with beer, feasts and dancing. But there was work for him still to do. Mujaji asked him if he would claim any reward; but he contented himself by telling her that if she would only allow him to accumulate his prize, and add it on to what he hoped would shortly be another award when he returned with the second medicine, then he would be able to claim a larger share of that which he desired.

"So he set out upon his second journey. His path led him westwards, over great mountains and across vast rivers, until in the end he reached a plain as flat as a shield, full of thornbush, and stretching from one horizon to the other.

"In this place dwelt the tribe of the Ndebele: a small, insignificant people, yet prosperous and with sleek women, colourfully dressed in many beads. They dwelt in a village which was as remarkable as themselves: a place with strange patterns and paintings on the walls, with passageways and huts of curious design.

"Thana found these people both friendly and hospitable. In the afternoon of the day of his arrival he was taken before their chief: an old man, blind, but of pleasant countenance and courteous manner. While the people crowded around their chief to hear the story, Thana spoke of the reason for his mission.

"At the end the chief considered the matter carefully.

"'You wish for the medicine of wisdom and cunning?' he asked. 'It is an ancient medicine, long used by our own fathers, and the only thing which has kept us, so weak a people, alive and wealthy in this world of barbarous and jealous men. It is true that we have a sufficiency of this medicine. It is compounded from two things: cunning, from the brain of a crocodile, which lives and prospers on others and cares not for their misery; and knowledge, from a mixture of the essences of earth and the perspiration of mankind. These things, mixed together, make the medicine you seek.

"'I am inclined to grant you the portion which you seek; and yet nothing is valued if it is too easily acquired. I will set you some slight task. In my old age and blindness my days pass slowly. He who lightens the passing of the hours with some jest or tale is rewarded. I will set you a problem. Tomorrow is our day for celebrating the first fruits of this season. For us it is a time of dancing, of song and feasting. Among our women there will be one on whose person will be hidden the medicine you seek. It will be where even I could find it, though I am without my sight. Find it, and the medicine is yours. But if you fail by sunset, then I shall hand you over to the women as a bondsman for a period, to do whatever is their bidding until you have earned your prize.'

"With that the chief withdrew and left Thana with the people, and the girls, who had many thoughts of those things which they would have him do.

"The day of festival was a day of beating drums and laughter, with beer and meat and singing, and all the people dressed in such elaborate fashion that Thana was half bemused by all he saw and heard. All morning he wandered among the women, eyeing them and trying to find which was the bearer of the medicine.

"There were young girls who giggled, and older girls who laughed, and still older ones who saw no further humour in man. By afternoon poor Thana was in a sad state of confusion. He withdrew and pondered closely on all the chief had told him, in the hope of finding some clue. Then he remembered that the chief had said that the bearer of the medicine would be one whom even he, in his blindness, could find.

"So Thana sat and watched the chief, to see how he would know a person; and when it chanced that the chief was alone for a little while, Thana ran to him and made as though to fasten his sandal, which was loose.

"'What is it?' asked the chief, startled.

"'Your sandal is loose,' mumbled Thana in a strange voice.

"The chief put out his hand to see who was there. He touched first Thana's head and then his face. Thana exulted. He completed his slight task and then hastened off. If the treasure was concealed on the person of a girl, and the chief could find her in an instant, then it must be somewhere on her head.

"Hastily he searched through the multitude of women. Time was short. He made his way from one group to another. There were heads thick, thin, long, round and fat. Then at last he found her. She was young and in her eyes was laughter, while her body was such that he had thought little of magic medicines when he had first seen her. On her head she wore a headdress of beads. Thana seized her in his eager hands, while she sought to run away. There, upon her head, concealed beneath the beads, was a tiny package; and he knew he had found that which the chief had so ingeniously hidden.

"Thana went his way in triumph. The Ndebele wished him well, for he was liked. The old chief gave him much advice about the dangers to be encountered on his way and he sped homewards, with many sighs from the girls behind him.

"At home Thana laid his treasure in Mujaji's hand, and the people greeted him as their hero. Once again there was feasting and dancing, and once again Mujaji asked him if he would choose his reward.

"Thana shook his head.

"'Work comes before delight,' he said; and although Mujaji agreed, she did so with regret, for even the flower fades while waiting for the bee to come to suck.

"Matala told Thana of his third task. It was the most arduous of all his missions.

"'In the north,' he said, 'much farther even than our ancient homeland, there lies a ruined city in a forest. In former times a certain king ruled there; but he was less interested in his people than in sorcery and forbidden learnings. So reckless did this monarch become that his people fled him in distaste, fearing that he had no desires but to debauch and kill.

"'Only the magicians and evil ones were left in this city; and in the course of years strange things took place in the precincts of that ruined place. Brute passions raged; and while the forest crept within the place, the men who dwelt there became half animal.

"'Stories have been told of vile deeds and practices in that lost town, and people have avoided it as they would a stinking corpse. And yet, it is there that the medicine of magic and transformation may be found. Go you, therefore, and secure this medicine; but this time do not travel alone, for the way is dangerous and long.'

"So Thana set out on his third mission, and five stalwart companions went with him on his way. Of their journey northwards through the bush I will not talk. Of its dangers, all I need tell you is that of the six who started out only four reached the banks of that great river which men call the Zambezi. Two died upon the way – a lion sprang upon one along the path, and the other was trampled to death by an elephant.

"Rain had delayed them for many days on their journey, and the river was running in a small flood when they reached its banks. They searched for a means to cross, for, no matter how weary one is, it is safer to sleep on the far side of any river, in case the flood grows worse during the night.

"By the banks, among the reeds, they found a dug-out canoe. In this, they made their way across the waters, with many alarms from the swirling floods before they reached the northern bank in safety. There they camped, and argued much all through the first half of the night. The journey had been more arduous than man can normally suffer; and the dangers that lay ahead seemed as many as the storm clouds upon the horizon of that summer sky.

"The three young men who escorted Thana had neither his strength of purpose nor his ambition, to act as a staff upon that dangerous way. They were afraid. That was no disgrace. Life was sweet to them, and there was no great purpose for which they were prepared to trade it. They wished to return, to obtain reinforcements perhaps, or devise some fresh expedient.

"Long they argued, while the night was restless and full of strange sounds, and the rumbling of the distant storm made a noise like many drums. At last they slept; but early in the dawn Thana's three companions stole away and left him sleeping there beside the dying fire.

"They took the canoe and launched themselves once more upon the waters; but the very danger they hoped to escape was waiting for them there on that great river. In the night the flood had worsened and brown waves of muddy water swept them down, with floating tree trunks and grass islands crowding all around them.

"Thana awoke to discover their absence. He ran to the banks, but there was nothing he could do to aid them. The river carried them down towards that place where it tumbles over a vast cataract, with spray rising to the heavens like a mighty smoke. There they died; and the river carried three corpses onwards for only a little while, before the crocodiles slid off the sandbanks and buried them in their foul stomachs.

"Thana went on his way alone and with a heavy heart. For many miles his path led him past the relics of ancient mines and towns long lost in ruin. On the twenty-seventh day he reached that evil city which lay brooding in the silence of the forest: a place malignant and full of menace.

"With care he made his way into the streets of that colossal wreck of past ages. What lay before him he little knew. He knew only that the magic which he sought was a lionskin cloak worn by those who lived within the city, who received strange powers of transformation from wearing it.

"Stone walls and towers and curious emblems lay strewn in ruination all around. Creepers grew upon the walls, and trees reached from the shadows to the sunshine. Stone steps twisted upwards, and corridors wound beneath tall walls. Owls flew from the darkness as he passed the houses. A cobra on a stairway reared its head and spat its hatred at him as he passed.

"No sign of man did he see. Yet, in some way, he knew that eyes were watching him closely. From a height a pebble came clattering down. Out of the corner of his startled eye he saw a figure vanish beyond a wall; but whether it was man or beast he could not say. He shouted and threw a stone; but there was no reply, save wondrous echoes up and down the streets.

"Behind a bush he glimpsed some figure staring at him; but it vanished before the stone he hurled could find its target. He turned a corner sharply and stood pressed into a niche, hoping that that which stalked him would walk into his trap. Instead, some figure beyond the further corner watched him until he felt its eyes groping as though into the secrets of his mind.

"With a shout he chased up the alley. The watcher vanished around the corner. Beyond it Thana found an empty passageway that ended in a door, heavy and solid and firmly closed. He ran and pounded on it. There was a great handle made of iron. He made to turn it, and then stopped to listen. From behind the door there came the sound of something breathing: a heavy, animal breathing, with a snarl of fury buried in it.

"Thana stood considering for a moment. He could not imagine what lay beyond the door; but if he was to obtain that which he desired it was needful to find out. If that which was concealed behind the door was as hostile as its breathing sounded, he would prepare some slight surprise for it. In a crevice of the paving stones he buried his spear, pointing at the doorway. Then, with his shield to cover him and a dagger in his hand, he opened wide the door.

"It was well that he was prepared. From the darkness beyond the door there came a lion. With fetid breath and hateful eyes, it sprang upon him in sullen rage. Thana fell back as he had planned, so that the spear fixed firmly in the ground reached up beside him, past his arm.

"The lion bore him down, with its paws upon his shield; but as it did so the spear penetrated deep within its chest. Loudly did it roar and dreadful was its pain. Beneath his shield Thana was soaked with the blood of the wild beast. Its fury was beyond control. It clawed him in the shoulder in its dying rage, and from behind his shield he looked deep into its yellow eyes and smelled its filthy breath. Then, to speed it on its way, he stabbed it in the heart with his dagger; and it died, half crushing him by its weight.

"Thana scrambled up. His shoulder was torn and bleeding, he was weak, and his mind was a whirl. Then, as he stared in horror at the monster, he saw it slowly change before his eyes from a beast into a man, who lay there dead with the spear in his lungs and a lionskin around his shoulders.

"It was then that Thana realised that this ruined city was the lair of that sect of lionmen who had been a curse in this vast land for long years past. He stripped the man of his lionskin cloak; and just in time. He heard a snarl. A second lion came bounding down the passageway towards him. He looked for escape. His spear was still wedged within the body of his victim. He had no defence.

"Behind him was the open door. He jumped within the passage and slammed the door shut behind him. He was just in time. The lion threw itself against the door with a crash. Thana raced on up the passage. A fresh snarl from in front brought him to a stop. A third lion was coming down towards him. He squeezed himself into a niche in the wall and held his breath. The new animal, fortunately, was intent on investigating the noise at the door. It raced past him and went on.

"Thana slipped out of the niche and ran up the passage. He turned a corner and to his relief saw the forest ahead. Within minutes he was out of that foul ruin. With one last glance behind him he fled into the forest, and did not cease running until he reached a stream, where he drank and rested by the waters to bathe his wound.

"It was not safe to linger at the stream. He splashed his way up its course for over a mile in order to leave no trail, and then turned aside into the bush and set his face for home.

"It was a bitter journey. He had obtained his treasure,

but his wounds were cruel. Indeed he would have died had not some old crone, a foolish thing who lived abandoned in the bush, found him once when he was delirious and fed him on berries and dressed his wounds with certain cooling herbs.

"In the end he saw once more the familiar hills and forests of his home. But this time there was no fond welcome. Mujaji's village lay in ruins. He walked into a place where only hyenas and vultures lived. The huts were burned, the corn bins looted, and the whole place littered with the bodies of many whom he had known and loved.

"In horror he searched the stricken place. There was no sign of Mujaji, but it was easy to see what tragedy had taken place. The bodies were not all those of Thana's own people. His comrades had not died without some fight. Among the dead lay many strange warriors, and from their costume and their tribal markings he knew them to be of the Swazi people.

"Thana hid the lionskin in the great cave, in the same place where lay the other hard-won medicines. Then he turned his face to the south and set off to the land of the Swazis, for he knew by the signs that some raiding band sent out by those martial people had attacked Mujaji, destroyed her town, and driven her and her surviving people off into captivity.

"We are now come very near the end of this story. Thana travelled down into the Swazi country, past vast mountains and a most beautiful waterfall. He found his way unharmed into the presence of the Swazi king, in the guise of a traveller craving hospitality.

"To the king, he told the story of his adventures and the weary miles he had travelled.

"'It is true', replied the king, at the end. 'I have this woman captive here, with some of her people. Know you that our seasons have been bad? At our first fruits' festival, the *incwala*, when the ancestors should send the rain to put out our fires, there was no more moisture than I have tears. Our doctors divined that this woman and you newcomers were an interference to the rains. So then we raided; and now we have her, and shall shortly send her spirit as a propitiatory present to our fathers.

"'That would be wrong', said Thana.

"'How so?'

"Thana argued long and well. He told the thoughtful Swazi king that she whom he held was really the queen of all the rain, and had lacked only the medicine. Now that she had the needful magics they held her captive. She could not use the medicines and there would be no rain.

"So, in the end, the king half believed him.

"'What I will do', he said, 'is let this woman free, with a few of her followers. But you and the others I will hold. She can work her magic where she wills; but if it rains not before this moon is out, you die with those others of her people – a few each day; and even she will not escape, for my arm is long.'

"'I am your man, and willing', answered Thana.

"So they released Mujaji, and Thana had only the chance to tell her of his last success and the place where he had hidden the skin. Then, with Matala and some few others, she sped on her way, for time was short and the magic must be made quickly to bring the rain.

"She went home to the ruined village, and there secured the three medicines for which Thana had sacrificed so much. With Matala, she spun her spells and made her secrets in that forest cave; but the rains came not. Day and night they worked, and tried variations of the ancient skills; but the moon waned and Mujaji's heart was sad, for she loved him who had already given her so much.

"And when the moon was dead, and the skies yet clear, she went in silence to the mountain top and there she wept, for her love was dead and all her hope was gone. And strange it was, that while she lay in sadness there and cried, her teardrops fell upon her magic. The rain gods came, thumping their shields, clashing their spears and sporting with one another in the skies.

"And behold, among the rain gods there was now a champion of Mujaji: a certain strong young spirit by the name of Thana, who loved her still, although his hunting grounds were now the skies.

"He forgets her not, nor she him. If she weeps for him and weaves her magic, Thana and the rain gods come. Still is it said, in times of drought, that Mujaji weeps for Thana, for her teardrops are the last magic of the rain. And because of her, he paints the sky afterwards with the emblazoned colours of his love, as a sign that he remembers her and has not failed; and while she still loves him he will protect her, even from that dread phantom – death."

"Was this the truth?" asked Bvekenya.

"Sir, these things are told by old people such as I. Each time the tales are told they vary in the telling. How am I to know what was in the beginning? That you must not ask. Was it good in the telling, or did you sleep? That is all that should concern you in a story such as this."

Bvekenya smiled.

"There was no sleeping; but now the night is old, and there is meat for all tomorrow. Let us rest."

So they slept, and it was in this way that Mgwazi told the hunters many stories during the time he travelled with them. When it rained he went off on his business. Only once more, years later, did Bvekenya see him again. Then he vanished. In some distant glade his bones must rest, while his spirit roams onwards in search of the last magic of the night. May he find it, for that magic is peace.

FOURTEEN

When the rains came

When the flamingoes flew westward Bvekenya knew that the drought was ending, for the rains were coming. The flamingoes had an uncanny knowledge of the weather. If it rained 500 miles away they would fly there with unerring instinct, in order to feed on the rich supplies of algae and animal life in newly flooded lakelets.

If the birds returned to their old haunts in the surrounding river swamps he would know that the distant rains had been insufficient; but if they stayed more than the few days' time required for their flight, then the rains were good and would surely soon spread eastwards to the parched bush.

As it happened, Bvekenya's stores were low when the flamingoes flew off. He decided to return to Makhuleke as quickly as possible for fresh provisions, before the rivers flooded and cut off all communications. With his hunters, donkeys and Yapie the mule, he followed the path and reached the little store safely.

He bought what was required and then turned back for the bush, hoping to be safe in his hunting grounds before the weather broke. Some of his Shanganes had lagged behind, shopping at the store. With two of his hunters, Bvekenya camped in the bed of the Limpopo River on the first night out, in order to allow the others to catch up. The river was completely dry. They had to dig a well eight feet down into the sand to find any water, and then it was muddy and half stagnant.

They had dug the well close to the bank of the river, just above its junction with the Pafuri, in the shade of a wild figtree. As sunset came, they were busy cooking their evening meal. Suddenly one of the Shanganes looked up and gave a startled shout. A wall of water close on ten feet high was sweeping down the riverbed, about half a mile away.

They jumped for their personal belongings. Fortunately they had simply bivouacked for the night and nothing was unpacked. Loaded with everything they could carry, they clambered up the riverbank. Behind them the river enveloped their former camp. Five minutes before they had laboured for one mug of dirty water: now, in an instant, a million gallons swept over their fire and cooking pots and washed all their remaining heavier goods away.

From the bank, they watched the water rushing past. The flood had no voice. It travelled, instead, in a silence which was terrible. It was brown, sullen and ruthless. It was laden with tree-trunks, drowned insects, and the wreckage of the crops of riverside farmers. Weaver birds' nests were scattered over its surface by the thousand. Flocks of birds wheeled overhead, some lamenting their fallen nests, others, such as the reckless forktailed drongos, snatching profit from destruction by diving for the half-drowned insects carried onwards by the flood.

Night was falling, and the hunters searched around for a camp. They pushed their way through the reeds and undergrowth tangled along the bank, and then received a shock. They were on an island in the river. The island was just an overgrown pile of sand, some twenty feet high and a hundred yards wide, offering only a precarious shelter in the midst of that raging flood.

The prospect was bleak. In the darkness they found the highest portion of the sandy island. There they pitched camp and made a fire. They had saved some salt, coffee and sugar from the flood; but all the other food was gone. They joked that at least they were no longer short of water. But when they filled their pot they found the water so thick with mud that it had the consistency of a foul-tasting mass of melted chocolate.

That night it rained, and all next day, and for two more days besides. It was misery. All the shelter they had was one canvas sail, held up by the branches of a thorn tree. Beneath it, Bvekenya and his two hunters sat huddled up, occasionally venturing out to examine the level of the waters.

Food was an immediate problem. As soon as the rain allowed them, they explored the island. They found a fair supply of cane-rats, while one or two small rietbok yielded them some venison. For vegetables they boiled the wild spinach (the *mvoba* plant) and found it good. For variety of diet they tried the frogs, for at least there were enough of them. The big bullfrogs were very tasty, like lobster; and a dozen or so for each man made quite an excellent dinner.

Only one mongrel dog had managed to reach the island with them. Yapie the mule had scrambled up to safety, but he did not take well to life on the island. Two days after the first flood he was wandering along the water's edge, searching for grazing, when a second and higher flood swept down. Poor Yapie was taken by surprise. With one loud bray, he was overwhelmed by the waters; and off he went, downstream, in the very midst of the flood waters.

The marooned party had one slight comfort. In one of his bags Bvekenya found a quantity of alum, which he always carried to purify water. This was a real godsend. They would boil the water, then put a pinch of alum in; and within ten minutes the mud would settle.

The amount of mud was astonishing. During the twenty-seven days they were marooned upon the island, Bvekenya experimented with the river to pass the time. Every day he boiled a paraffin tin of water for drinking purposes. Then he collected the mud deposited by the alum. At the same time he measured the average flow of the river. By throwing a stump into the water and running beside it on the bank, he found it was flowing at the rate of one hundred yards a minute.

The river was 300 yards wide and twelve feet deep. From the amount of mud accumulated by the alum, he worked out that the silt carried by the river amounted to no less than fourteen pounds of good earth per cubic yard of water.

Of course, this was an exceptional flood. The Shanganes reckoned it was the greatest flood in thirty years, and they were certainly not far wrong.

Watching the flood waters swirling past was a fascinating pastime. All manner of birds wheeled and called above the waters. The flood had dislocated their lives as much as it had Bvekenya's. Food was the craving of everything, for the mud and the velocity of the current prevented the river birds from fishing.

Bvekenya was sitting on the bank once, watching the flood and cutting a rietbok into biltong. He had a nice length of meat skewered on a stick, when suddenly the mongrel dog leaped in and snatched it from him. One of the Shanganes, still a youth, tore after the dog. He retrieved the meat. Then, as he ran after the dog, the meat held up above him, a hungry kite swooped down with great daring and seized the disputed item.

The kite flew up in triumph; but there were other watching eyes besides Bvekenya's. A white-headed fish eagle swooped down upon the kite and robbed it of its prize. Up went the eagle; and then its mate, who had been watching, dived upon it with a harsh cry and tried to relieve it of its booty.

In the air above the river a short and vicious battle raged. Then the meat was dropped. Both eagles dived in an effort to retrieve it. Both fought to retard the other, and so lost their chance. There was still another hungry watcher of that one piece of meat. As it reached the surface of the river a crocodile, lying unobserved but seeing all, snapped it up with his steel jaws and vanished below the surface.

The crocodiles hated the floods as much as any other creatures. Instinct, or their wonderful hearing, always seemed to warn them in good time of the rising waters. They clambered out and found a sanctuary in the reeds, or in some sheltered backwater where they could lurk, roaming the banks for food, venturing for miles from the river, like raiding pirates forced on land by some storm upon the ocean.

The hippos also had their lives confused by the raging of the waters. For creatures of their bulk to be caught in a wild torrent of water could mean complete disaster. Like the crocodiles, they sought to escape by finding sanctuary on the banks, or in some shallow backwater.

Once, in the Lundi River, twenty miles below the pools at Tshipinda, one hippo bull was caught by the avalanche of water. He was overwhelmed and literally buried alive beneath an enormous mass of reeds. Months later, while Bvekenya was there, a veld fire spread into this pile of reeds lying alongside the river. When the fire was over he found the body of the hippo and, without shedding any tears, still was sorry at the manner of the animal's passing.

The floods always brought down vast quantities of debris. Enormous trees would come sailing down, and often some alarmed snake would be seen among the branches, being carried off to what everyone hoped would be an unpleasant end.

These distressed reptiles were an embarrassment on the island. Many of them managed to wriggle ashore and became most unwelcome companions.

Once Bvekenya was lying dozing on the banks, lulled half asleep by the gurgling of the waters. He was just embarked on pleasant dreams when he felt something move through the grass beside him. He opened his eyes and lifted his head. There was a twelve-foot-long black mamba in the grass beside him.

He lay petrified. A snake will invariably bite as a reaction to any sudden move. Fear, therefore, is a negative defence, for it makes the victim stay dead still.

The snake crawled leisurely over Bvekenya's chest and lay there, lifting its head from this vantage point and looking about, quite unaware of any human presence. It was agony. Every second was a long one. Perspiration was pouring out of Bvekenya and trickling down his face with a maddening tickle. He saw the snake in astonishing detail: its cold, still eyes, its forked tongue, the deathly shape of its head.

Then there was a step in the grass. From nearby came the voice of one of his Shanganes.

"Sir, here are some berries for you."

The snake twisted in an instant and was gone. As for Bvekenya, the shadow of death had touched him and it was cold.

The debris carried by the flood did not only bring unpleasant companions to the island, but, in the end, brought rescue as well. Three weeks after the first flood, still a third wave of water came down the river, bringing with it vast masses of reeds and palm leaves. This debris piled up on the banks of the islands and gave Bvekenya the idea of making some sort of raft or boat.

One essential item in Bvekenya's camp equipment was always a canvas sail. It was ubiquitous in its usefulness. In travelling it was used as a saddle cloth, while on long, dry treks it could be turned into a spare water container by being rubbed with fat and twisted into two bundles on either side of a donkey's back. In camp it became a roof supported by branches, and now he perfected a method of using it to ford rivers, which he remembered and found useful during all his years in the bush.

From the reeds washed up on the island, he built a frame. This he covered with the sail, and then launched himself upon the water. For a paddle he used an enamel plate. He drilled small holes on the lips of the plate and to these tied the split end of a stick. He thus had a combined paddle and oar, which gave him good momentum. In after years he developed his boating technique still further, by pulling a donkey or mule into the water and holding the animal tightly with its legs underneath the back of the little canvas boat. The animal would then swim behind the boat, pushing it along, while Bvekenya steered and could guide the donkey-powered liner past sandbanks, sunken tree trunks, hippos, and eventually select some suitable landing point on the opposite bank.

In a boat such as this, Bvekenya managed to leave the river island. He rescued his Shanganes and they returned to the comforts of Makhuleke, with no regrets at leaving their precarious sandbank sanctuary.

Bvekenya's only serious loss, apart from some stores and personal goods, seemed to have been Yapie the mule. There was no sign of that perky little animal; and, with regret, he was given up as dead. But months later, when Bvekenya was back in the bush, he received a message from Buck Buchanan of Makhuleke. Yapie had been found again. He was living the life of a sort of mule-Robinson Crusoe on another island lower down the river, at the junction of the Limpopo and the Pafuri. He must have scrambled ashore on this island as the flood carried him past. It was a larger island than Bvekenya's sanctuary, and the grazing was ample to keep the mule alive. Bvekenya eventually retrieved him safe and sound, and none the worse for his months of beachcomber existence.

The erratically destructive nature of the great Limpopo is a byword among the people who live on its banks. It is a river of almost as many names as it has moods, and most of them refer to its violence. The name Limpopo or *iliMphopho* is a legacy of the Matebele, and indicates a river of sudden rises, falls and powerful flow. The Venda know it as *Vhembe*, meaning "The Gatherer", while the Shanganes call it *Methe* or "The Swallower", from a similar idea of the river's destructive habit of gathering, swallowing, and destroying all life along its banks.

The river, of course, is not always violent. At times it is beautiful beyond compare. It is then that the waters seem languid and sultry: flowing lazily, mile after mile, through a green forest of giant trees, whose longest boughs often meet across the river from opposite banks.

The riverside forests are always the most beautiful in Africa. Giant *hlaru* trees send their graceful traceries of leaves and branches upwards in complex patterns. Groves of spectral fever trees stand whispering together in the hollows. *Mtoma* trees loom protectively over glades of green-blue shadows, deliciously cool in the summer heat, while all around a host of other great trees stand in tangled ranks along the water's edge, their leaves playing in the winds and their roots festooned about the eroded banks.

In spring this riverside wilderness is at its best. It is then that the air is heavy with the perfume of the *nkayi* trees, all richly gowned with pure white blossoms, like brides dressed for marriage with that gallant youth – summer.

All the trees of the wilds have come to their wedding. They stand peering over one another's shoulders to see the bridal party. The placid river is the brown carpet that leads them to the altar; and in these months of spring its whole surface for five hundred miles is still strewn with the floating confetti of autumn's golden leaves.

The *mvimbangwenya* trees are among the most enthusiastic of the wedding guests. Their puffy little bright-yellow flowers are strewn so liberally over the river that in places the Limpopo is completely covered.

The *mvimbangwenya* is an oddly named tree. The name means "that which stops the crocodiles". It is said that when the tree is in flower the crocodiles are vicious and hungry for man. When the flowers are over the crocodiles are subdued and harmless, so the presence of even a single blossom on the water is regarded by the Shanganes as a sure warning of death concealed by the slightest ripple.

Another odd river-dweller is the dark green *phalavurha* shrub. It is a willowy version of the ubiquitous wild fig, which lines the very edge of the river densely, as though planted there by the green fingers of Providence, to protect the banks from the erosion of the floods. The *phalavurha* has a most remarkable leaf. It is a rough, natural sandpaper. The name *phalavurha* means "that which smooths the bow", and its leaves are used to impart the final polish to the Shanganes' bows and arrows.

The lovely river wilderness has a tranquillity which is more illusionary than real. Beneath the surface of the waters, and in the bush along the banks, endless warfare rages.

Every length of *phalavurha* bush conceals some crocodile, hippo or leguaan. Even the waterside trees themselves know little security in what should be their especial paradise. On all sides may be seen signs of the river's violent temper. Great trees have been torn down and block the waterway, while others cling despairingly to all that remains of what was once a solid portion of the bank, but has long since been undermined and washed away.

Beneath the surface of the waters there is as little security as above. Innumerable fish – fat, bewhiskered barbel, and the vicious tiger fish – feel rather than see their way through the muddy waters. Occasionally one rises to the surface with a sudden flurry and splash. Perhaps it has been attracted by a fly or insect; but more likely some strange terror deep down in the turgid waters has sent it jumping for its life, with the jaws of a crocodile or otter only a few inches behind.

Perhaps it is the birds who are happiest in the riverside forest. Certainly, a whole multitude of the feathered fraternity make their homes in the trees, the reeds and the overhanging shrubs.

Every overlooking cliff is riddled with the little cave-like nests of *Nkhota*, the white-fronted bee-eater, while the complex nests of the weaver birds sway over the water from the extremist tips of the riverside trees.

Brilliantly coloured kingfishers dart from bank to bank, each preoccupied on some busy task. The wise old hammerheads probe about with their long beaks and hungry eyes, investigating every hiding place of frogs or crabs or fish; and those odd characters, the stilts, with their long, red, stilt-like legs, stalk along in the shallows searching the mud for food.

A flock of egrets, like so many enormous white blossoms, sit preening on an overhanging bough with the water beneath them to serve as a mirror. The white-headed fish eagles perch aloofly on the tops of the highest trees, like sentries forever on the watch. Parties of the noisy hadedah ibis go racing up the river with the reckless raucousness of a crowd of young bloods speeding homewards from a dance.

More tranquil by far are the wild geese and ducks, gliding leisurely over the waters. Perhaps a pair of Egyptian geese will sail along beside the bank, keeping to the shallows with their compact little huddle of goslings swimming beside them, playing with reflections, darting off to catch some fly or tiny fish, and seemingly safe from the attentions of the crocodiles through some age-old pact.

From the banks, at times, comes that curious sound: the *"Houm, Houm-Houm: Houm, Houm-Houm,"* of the grave turkey buzzards or ground hornbills, rummaging about in the bush in twos or threes like preoccupied prospectors endlessly searching for gold.

More welcome, perhaps, is the sharp, insistent *"Chi-Chi-Chi-Chi-Chi"* of the honey guides: those cunning little birds which seek to attract the attention of man or honey badger, offering to lead them, in exchange for a share in the booty, to some store of honey. Their persistence is such that many a hunter has been forced to abandon his quarry and follow the bird, if only to silence its chatter.

But to what a prize the bird will often serve as guide! To some place where the bees drowse in the heat, their hives, in a tree-trunk or crevice, dripping with a honey which captures and solidifies the very essence of all the colour and the scent, the warmth and the flavour, of the African wilds.

The riverside forest is as favourite a home for animal life as it is for the birds. Every overlooking hillock or cliff is the home of the nimble klipspringer, the antelope mountaineer who has for so long found sanctuary on the most inaccessible rock faces. Every tree seems to be the home for some baboon or troop of monkeys, gambolling along the water's edge and occasionally scampering into shelter with a furious alarm when a martial eagle zooms menacingly down the long green valley formed by the trees growing along the riverbanks.

A whole tangle of pathways leads the creatures of the wilds down to the river to drink. Each pathway finds its end at some gap in the bank leading to shallow water, or a sandbank upon which the game animals can stand, finding, it would seem, as much pleasure from the sight of the river with the sunset or the moonlight on its waters as they do from their long, cool drinks.

The footprints at these drinking places have many stories to tell. There are the nervous tracks of the impala herds; and the nyala: the handsome, bearded males with their demure females, surely the most beautiful of antelope.

There are the heavy, restless pads of the hyenas, the mobile cemeteries of the wilds, in whose tomblike stomachs all things, sooner or later, seem to end. The erratic, excitable tracks of the jackals; the sly, furtive pads of the leopards; the deep, purposeful trail of the lions; the giant pads of the elephants, who always walk in the middle of the way and shoulder all others apart: all these may be found at the drinking places by the banks of the river.

No man can tell of the sights the old river must see in its long journey to the sea. There must be long lonely stretches, where the river is deep and turgid and nothing disturbs the silence save the splash of a crocodile. There must be warm and languid stretches where the hippos laze in the shallows, with the little calves sleeping in security on their mothers' backs.

There must be sudden rapids and falls, where the fish fight to make their way upstream. There must be sinister stretches, with the river choked by tangled vegetation and blocked by fallen trees.

There must be nightmare stretches, past haunted islands; sinister sandbanks covered with reeds, shrubs, and wreckage carried down by the floods, providing a secure home for *Hlathu*, the python, who loves to lie submerged in the shallows to cool during the slow process of digestion, or lay eggs on the islands and coil up around them, a fifteen-foot length of muscle, with no love for the offspring but with an ingrained instinct to protect the eggs while the sun warms them slowly into life.

There must be countless miles where the reflections play with the ripples, where moonlight laughs upon the surface, and where the end of the rainbow rests. There must be high banks, where the hippos scramble up muddy slides. There must be fording places where the crocodiles lie in wait with the patience of death. There must be islands where no man has ever trodden, all overgrown with a green and tangled forest; lonely villages must lie so close to the river's edge that the sounds of laughter and hate, or the beating of drums, drift down and merge with the gurgling of the waters.

All these things – beautiful, sinister, happy, fearful and sad – the river sees on its journey. As the current gathers strength from its tributaries, so the river's unfathomable nature gathers all the moods, thoughts and wondrous wisdom of Africa and its mysterious ways; and then it glides, as life should glide into death, serene and noble, to lose its waters, its dreams and itself in the unfathomable depths of the ocean.

FITTEEN
The blackbirders

T here were many ways, other than hunting, of making money in the bush. Admittedly, few of them were honest ways; but in a society where money is generally the excuse for the manner of its making, and greater commercial value is placed on cunning than intelligence, who can blame the bushrangers such as Bvekenya for resorting to odd stratagems and schemes?

Some of the honest ways of making money wilted in the harsh environment of the bush, like hothouse orchids planted in a rockery. Bvekenya tried to cultivate several of these delicate blooms, but soon found that the more hardy, if sometimes thorny, shrubs stood a better chance of flourishing.

About 1915, one optimistic soul named Hendrik Hartman came to Makhuleke. He met Bvekenya at the store and the two men decided on a joint venture. Behind the Soutpansberg on the Brak River lay vast areas of open land which Hartman considered ideal for sheep. The arrangement they reached was that Bvekenya would obtain sheep on his travels to Rhodesia and drive them down to Makhuleke, where Hartman would take over and, when stocks were sufficient, move the herd off to grazing grounds behind the Soutpansberg.

Bvekenya collected about six hundred head, and Hartman was prepared to leave after the next batch was brought in. How often is it that the one more thing – the extra pound man always hopes for – is the finish of him?

Bvekenya arrived with fifty sheep and found Hartman missing. The Shanganes told him that his partner had gone off early that morning with a hatchet and the declared intention of cutting thorn trees to provide material for a bigger sheep pen.

Bvekenya waited until evening. When the darkness came, he decided it was time to search for Hartman. He set off, firing an occasional round into the air as a signal to his partner. Presently he heard a faint shout. He made his way in the direction of the sound. He reached a large *nkayi* tree, whose knobbly thorns made its branches ideal for use as a protective hedge around livestock or a camp.

Perched on one of the uppermost branches was Hartman. Around the tree lay a pile of lopped-off branches. The man had busied himself in cutting branches off the tree, carefully leaving just sufficient to allow him to descend; but when he tried to reach the ground he found the pile of fallen branches was ten feet high and so tangled that he was truly hedged in.

Hartman had sat in the tree all day, shouting for help; but nobody had come to aid him. Robbed of shade by his own industry, he had been exposed to the full heat of a scorching sun. When Bvekenya freed him from his curious prison, he had sunstroke and a high fever.

Bvekenya summoned the Shanganes and they carried Hartman to the store. There they supplied him with such comforts as they had; but he died the next day, and actually became the occupant of that quiet corner of the local cemetery which William Pye had long before promised to Bvekenya.

Bvekenya now found himself landed with the sheep, and no clear idea of what to do with them. Living in Crooks

Corner was a Welshman, named Theodore Williams by his parents but better known locally by his African name of *Makhanda*. Williams had run some sheep in Crooks Corner, but every animal had died. The pens and runs he had constructed, however, remained; and Bvekenya decided that the thing to do was to use them.

He went back to the bush to resume his hunting. Soon a message reached him that the sheep were dying fast. He returned to Makhuleke, with a few goats he had bartered on the journey to serve as food. He found that over half the sheep had died. He drove his goats into the kraal. They seemed notably unwilling, but he assumed that they were just unused to any form of containment.

He went into the adjoining hut to unpack. Ten minutes later his Shanganes came running to tell him that one of the goats had died. Bvekenya went into the kraal himself to inspect the goat. The place was alive with fleas. Millions and millions of them were jumping about the dry floor of that long disused pen with its wall of thorns. The goat had been eaten alive. No wonder the dogs, cats, the fowls and sheep, were all dead or dying in that hideous place.

Bvekenya rescued four hundred of his sheep. The rest, with all their lambs, had died. Williams was away, but Bvekenya set his whole establishment on fire and watched with delight as the fleas jumped in the centre of the pen, trying to escape the flames creeping upon them from the surrounding thorns.

Theodore Williams was a blackbirder by profession. It was an interesting occupation, and very profitable if properly managed. From the very beginning of mining in Southern Africa, in the wild days of the first great rush to Kimberley, an insatiable demand had arisen for labour.

At first the miners depended upon the rewards they offered to attrack their workers. The tribal African in the bush was hardly interested in the idea of removing himself permanently from his habitual life in the wilds to some slum which acted as a housing-adjunct to a mine or factory. But he was susceptible to the idea of temporary migrant labour, where he could earn a few pounds to tide him over a lean season at home, aid him to obtain the necessary funds to cover the *lobolo* (bride price) of a wife, or provide the cash to pay some tax imposed upon him by his government.

So, in the course of years, the migrant labour system developed; and tribesmen tramped for thousands of miles along the paths, through all manner of perils and hardships, so that they could reach a place of work and there earn a trifling amount of cash, and possibly an old muzzle-loader or gaspipe gun, with some powder and a few lumps of lead or iron to be beaten into bullets.

With the discovery of gold in the Transvaal, the demand for labour reached fantastic proportions. Mine owners were no longer content just to sit and wait for a haphazard flow of labour, and they stimulated the idea of systematic recruitment. They offered what was known as a capitation fee to whoever would recruit workers and present them to the mines or their representatives. The capitation fee, in Bvekenya's time, amounted to £7 a head for an adult, £4 for a youth, and £1 for a boy. This was almost as much as the workers were likely to earn themselves during a normal period of employment.

No particular questions were asked as to the origin or manner of enlistment of the Africans. The prospects, there-fore, of making rapid fortunes as professional recruiters of labour (blackbirders, as they were called) became apparent to many; and a stream of men made their way into those territories where there was a large primitive population.

Bvekenya had met many of these blackbirders in the course of his first few years in the bush. One of the first recruiters in his part of the world after the Anglo-Boer War had been the Australian Jack Ford, a former Rhodesian policeman who had subsequently bought the store at Ma-khuleke.

Jacob Martin Diegel (known as Charlie to the Shanganes) was another of the fraternity, while John Dart, a Welshman; Wieder, a Hungarian; and a Swede named Colesen ran a blackbirding syndicate.

Jack Lambart was another individual who came recruiting, but he did not last long. He would recruit a few Shanganes, collect his fees, and then get blind drunk. Generally he would wander off into the bush to sober up. He did that once too often and was seen no more. Maybe a lion found him lying beneath a tree and proved a more terrible companion than any pink elephant.

Many other odd characters arrived in the bush, for, superficially, recruiting seemed an easy way of making money and was so general that even magistrates or game rangers would often privately give a prisoner the option of gaol or enlistment, so that they could have the fee.

A strange individual named Johnson once walked into Bvekenya's camp, followed by a Shangane servant leading a pack donkey. Johnson was straight from town. He was immaculately dressed in a smart blue suit with white collar and tie. He arrived almost dead from hunger. Bvekenya, as it happened, was feasting at the time on a fat eland cooked with sweet potatoes. He saw in his surprise guest a reminder of himself in his early days. He dined the man to capacity, then stuffed the pockets of his new suit with venison and sweet potatoes and watched him on his way with wonder. How long the stranger lasted Bvekenya never knew, but he saw him no more.

The technique followed by the recruiters varied considerably. Some confined themselves to tramping along the paths, visiting the various kraals and talking to the tribespeople, propagandising the money, adventure and food to be found at the mines. Any tribesmen who enlisted would then be stood a square meal on the spot, for from the moment a man enlisted he was the responsibility of his particular recruiter; and besides, the occular demonstration of a generous meal invariably impressed other individuals with the advantages of signing on. In this manner, the recruiter would make his way to a whole succession of kraals. If he was lucky, an increasingly long line of recruits would trudge along behind him, being fed and carefully tended until the recruiter eventually returned to his base, where he could trade them for cash.

This was the ideal type of recruiting, as visualised in the fond dreams of mine owners speaking at social functions, or in the writings of journalists paid by the newspapers the magnates owned.

Often recruiting was, in fact, carried out along those lines; but too often the recruiter was a drunken scoundrel who would resort to the most infamous means of securing "boys". The methods of these individuals were generally on a par with those employed by the naval press gangs in the days of old. The bushrangers were as tough a crowd as any bully bosun. They asked no quarter from life, and gave none. Black ivory was a trade commodity to them, and they would utilise every dodge to obtain it. They would rob others of their recruits by force, terrorise a district; corrupt degenerate chiefs into coercing their people – and generally make a curse of themselves to the whole countryside.

The best time to recruit was in the years of drought. If there was hunger in the land the men would steadily slip away to work, leaving their women behind to eke out some sort of miserable existence on roots and berries.

A man would never tell his women he was going, for fear they would bewitch him. It was customary for him to run away from home, for the women would always struggle to detain him; and when the crops failed, and recruiting was in the air they would keep a very close eye on all eligible males.

Some tribesmen enlisted over and over again, and were more often away from home than there. Most enlisted for a period of 360 shifts at a time, in which case they would be away for up to fifteen months. They would earn about £3 a month and their keep. The great majority took their payment in a lump sum at the end of their contract. From this sum would be deducted sundry expenses of transport, and such taxes as the individual had owing to his government. With the balance the man was free to return home, although recruits of the Portuguese received half their wages on their own side of the border.

It was the triumphant return home which was, of course, the climax of the mine labourers' lives. They loved to return after the rains, when crops, food and beer would be plentiful, and have a final thrill in the fording of some swollen river.

They would walk back importantly into the old home village, with a load of fancy clothes and gewgaws for their womenfolk. They would sit down without a word and expect to be petted and flattered and wheedled to recount the details of their adventures.

Then, at last, almost reluctantly, would come the story of their adventures, told in the minutest detail; and it was for this thrill of being the centre of attraction, the storyteller of the kraal, that many men enlisted.

All brought a remarkable story home with them. When they had started they were *Momparas* (bumpkins) or New Ones. Now they were *Magayisas* or Rich Ones, laden with experience, anecdote and gifts for every member of the family.

They would tell how they had fooled everyone and stolen away to enlist. They had tramped along the paths; fallen trees had barred their way; wild animals had menaced them. They had seen the trails of the supernatural beasts upon the pathway.

Then, at last, they had reached the recruiter's camp. The recruiter was a famous man. He had fed them well on this and that and so many times a day, and the meat was fat or lean. Other men had trooped in from foreign lands, beyond even the great Zambezi.

They had become a whole gang of recruits. They had moved south of a mysterious line called the 22°, for it was so ordered by the whites that nobody could be recruited north of that degree of south latitude. But their recruiter was wise. He had certain chiefs who received from him many presents.

These chiefs now agreed to call the recruiter's men their own. They had been instructed about these chiefs and even taught, parrot-like, a few words of the chief's strange language. They were even given a pound to pay tax and get a new pass from a Portuguese policeman. Then they had been delayed, for some were more stupid than others in learning how to lie well. But at last they had gone on to Makhuleke, where lay a compound for them to sleep in, and where their recruiter had handed them over to the trader with much counting, first of them, and then of sovereigns.

Then they had gone to Louis Trichardt or Soekmekaar. There the doctor examined them, and off they went by train to the golden Rand. Immense detail followed, of how they had travelled by train, how they had reached Johannesburg station, how an imposing Zulu boss-boy in a uniform had met them there. How he had led them out of the station like a goat leading sheep.

How they had suddenly passed from the gloom of the station into the clamour, light and movement of Eloff Street, Johannesburg. How they had followed the boss-boy through the streets, with their eyes full of numb terror at the strangeness of the fantastic modern world around them.

And then their experiences on the mines. First of all the food, its quantity and quality. Then their white masters, how they spoke and whether they were kind or brutal. And the odd names these white men gave them: Sikkies, Knife,

Fife, Doek, Fifteen, Watch, Sockies, Nelson, Wellington, Bottle or Damnfool.

Details of the work, on the surface or six thousand feet or more down at the bottom of an incredible shaft, were the most difficult of all for the returned mineworker to tell. The average migrant labourer had a somewhat circumscribed idea, to say the least, of the vast juggernaut of the mining industry. He was the lowliest, but yet the most important figure in the whole colossal enterprise. He was one of a million other tiny gears, all turning an immense machine; and he rotated strictly on a most confined axis, with scant appreciation of the overall plan or the cumulative effect of his labours.

His description of work, therefore, sounded to the sophisticated like somebody describing with a wealth of detail a pimple on an elephant, rather than the whole animal itself. Perhaps he had worked a drill, or shovelled rocks in one position for fifteen months. Perhaps he had worked in the mill, in the midst of its shattering, ear-splitting, never-ending roar. Perhaps he had lain flat on his back in a hole dug out beneath the coco-pan rails, and for fifteen months had the single task of daubing grease on the axles of the cars as they passed overhead. If this had been his job – a classic occupation indeed in the midst of the golden Rand – then the simple soul probably still looked the part, with grease clinging to his person from as far back as his first day's work.

Then came the great day, when he set off for home. On the way to the mines he had been dressed in skins, and perhaps a few scanty rags, with all his personal belongings, some scraps of food, and a calabash of water tied on a stick and carried over his shoulder in a net of rushes.

Returning, he was rich. New jerseys, emblazoned with football colours; new loincloths; stylish hats or gaily coloured scarves; gaudily decorated tin or wooden trunks packed with blankets and cloth for his women – and, glory of glories, perhaps a concertina, fiddle or guitar with which to strum a single simple harmony for hundreds of miles, while he tramped towards home with his trunk upon his back and his tongue hanging out from heat and thirst.

The persistence of these homeward bound magayisas was often startling. Bvekenya met one once, a hundred miles from nowhere, struggling along the path carrying a large grandfather clock. Every mile or so he would sit down with his companions to rest. He would solemnly start the clock and, along with any casual passers-by, sit open-mouthed waiting for the chimes.

Bvekenya asked him what he intended to do with this strange object.

"It will tell my wife when to feed me," the magayisa replied with simple joy.

Just how many of these migrant labourers left home and never returned is a story that remains unwritten. Many of those that did return were robbed of their hard-won money by some European or African scoundrel – the lowest of all footpads – who lay in wait for them along the way.

Others came back to curious and most poignant tragedy. There was one man, a Shangane from Garakwe's country, north of the Great Save. He saw a girl once, washing in the shallows of a pleasant stream, and from that moment he loved her dearly.

He had little wealth, but he courted her and she soon loved him. He paid her parents all he had, £2 on account, and then tramped off to earn the balance of the bride price on the mines.

He worked hard and well, saved his money with religious care, and then returned home full of love and happiness. He found the girl, strong and lovable and waiting for him. For such a girl her parents demanded £30; but he paid it willingly, although the price was high.

A fine new hut was built, standing high on stilts, like all the others in the neighbourhood, for the lions were very bold and of infamous appetite in that district, and the village had been pestered with maneaters for some time.

To this place the groom took his young bride, and derived great joy from presenting her with all the trinkets and gifts he had carefully reserved for this time of happiness. Then he took her in his arms, and all night they lay in sweet delight, with the firm ripeness of her breasts pressed close against his chest.

With the warning of the first dawn, they felt great thirst, for their passion had been a fever. She went out to fetch a calabash of water for her love. She was a very young bride, and in the excitement of the marriage day she had forgotten certain things. The water had been left in calabashes on the ground below the hut.

She looked down in the dim light and saw that all was quiet and the shadows were without movement. She went down the ladder to the ground and stooped to fetch the water. From the darkness there came a lion, black-maned and savage. He snapped her backbone as though it was a twig. His cruel teeth cut through her breasts and she knew no more of the pleasure, the loves and the pangs of this life.

Above, in the hut, her husband wept in anguish as that great hunter, the sun, rose over the far Indian Ocean and sent his shafts of light probing into the shadows to hunt down the wild beast of the night.

As for the lions, they terrorised the village for months until a blackbirder, one of the most notorious of his kind, Thomas Adams by name, arrived and took pity on the people. Night after night he sat on the platform of one of the stilt huts with a pile of meat next to him. Every time he saw a lion move, the surprised animal received manna from heaven in the form of a chunk of meat delicately flavoured with arsenic. In this way Adams poisoned all the maneaters and made himself some lifelong friends among the villagers.

Bvekenya had soon become involved in the recruiting business, for its profits were too tempting to miss for anybody in the bush. Especially after the collapse of the sheep venture with Hartman, he developed the trade in black ivory until it surpassed by far the profits he made from tusks. But whether profit came his way from hunting elephants or blackbirding labour was a matter of indifference, for both meant fortune on the ivory trail.

Bvekenya developed his recruiting into a major business. He blazed new paths and built permanent camps for his recruits at each of the water-holes. He established some camps even in the immediate vicinity of Portuguese posts: small, surreptitious affairs, hidden in dense bush, their vicinity indicated to those in the know by means of a secret code of markings scratched into the nearby paths.

The very reputation Bvekenya had acquired acted as his greatest aid in recruiting. He was so well known in the bush by then that few Shanganes cared to risk his displeasure by signing on with a rival.

Also Bvekenya, in his rough way, did his best to help his recruits, both going and coming from the mines. His prowess with the rifle guaranteed them food. His reputation guaranteed them some protection from the footpads, and one of his special inducements to recruits was actually the means of saving many lives.

The reason recruitment of labour from areas north of the 22° of south latitude had been prohibited was the high mortality rate of Africans from the tropics. Countless thousands of recruits from these northern areas died of pneumonia before the prohibition was enforced in October 1913.

Then the smuggling started, for the recruiters mostly could not care less whether the labourers lived or died, and the mines were not unduly particular. Bvekenya joined willingly in the smuggling, and, in fact, was its greatest exponent. He had a whole string of chiefs in the south, suitably corrupted to the tune of £1 per recruit; and they would pass the foreign men off as their own blood and tribe.

What saved the lives of Bvekenya's tropical men was the present he gave to each recruit of a singlet, blanket and loincloth. This warm clothing, and the slow rate of travelling along Bvekenya's secret paths, plus the time they spent learning the lies they must tell to change their identity, allowed the tropical men time to acclimatise themselves and prepare for the cold air of the mines on the highveld. By these means Bvekenya computed that only 3% of his illegal tropical recruits failed to return, compared to the 25% who died when they were sent down in the legitimate manner – by sea to Lourenço Marques and from thence by train to the highveld.

Bvekenya's rise from the ranks to the notoriety of Africa's leading illegal recruiter was not achieved without friction with his rivals. All the blackbirders had touts out trying to enrol recruits and clashes often occurred. Gangs of recruits being sent in by one blackbirder would be waylaid by the touts of a rival. Long tales would be spun of how the mine to which they were going was a hideous sweatshop, while the tout's own master was an agent for paradise. Whole gangs would disappear in this fashion and sign up with somebody else.

Bvekenya had one big party of tropical recruits on the way to the Pietersburg depot in 1913. When they arrived, the prohibition had just been introduced and the authorities refused to admit them. The recruits dispersed in dismay. Local recruiters immediately collected them, taught them their parrot-like stories of a change of address, and next day successfully handed them in. Bvekenya lost over £700 on that deal, and he never forgot it.

Some time later he sent twenty more recruits down to Crooks Corner from the Save. Colesen, the Swede, met them on the path and told them the story of his paradise mine, and the death-trap where Bvekenya was sending them.

It was quite a few months afterwards that Bvekenya went down to Makhuleke store. On the ridge where the store was built he met the Swede.

"Well, Bvekenya," said the Swede – a big, brawny sort of man. "I fooled you then. I scared your boys. I'll fool you again and scare away some more; and what are you going to do about it, hey?"

Bvekenya stamped on the thick Swedish toes. Colesen looked down. Bvekenya let drive with an uppercut that connected all the way. The Swede's nose dissolved into something like a saucer of beetroot. He stood bemused.

"What is it?" he asked dully, feeling his nose.

"Your nose is busted," said Bvekenya.

The Swede let out a delayed bellow of terror and pain. Behind him stood his cart, with two mules outspanned and tied to the shaft. His howl would have awakened the dead in the graveyard of Crooks Corner, let alone the two mules. With a snort they tore off. Colesen ran one way and the mules another, with the cart bumping off behind them. They raced down the slope of the ridge. They crashed through a goat kraal and into a crowd of Shanganes cooking food behind a reed fence.

The Shanganes scattered. The cart overturned and the mules broke free. Colesen, Shanganes, mules and cart were all heading in different directions. Bvekenya had lost £140 in Colesen's little *hebe* (or "scaring away") but he had no further trouble from his rivals. Most of them gave up in despair and left the bush to Bvekenya. In 1917 alone, his best year, he recruited 3250 Africans illegally and safely smuggled them past Portuguese and Transvaal police alike, along the secret paths which were his own black ivory trail.

SIXTEEN

My gun is my friend

Early in 1918 Bvekenya was at Crooks Corner, visiting William Pye. Conflicting rumours of the course of the First World War had disturbed the bushrangers for some time. Bvekenya had combined business with a desire for news and had tramped in from the bush to Makhuleke. William Pye was always the most loquacious of the local inhabitants, and that afternoon they were gossiping together of bush life in general and the war in particular.

There was a knock on the door.

"Open it," said Pye: "It'll be Buck, he said he'd come down."

Bvekenya opened the door. There were two Rhodesian policemen standing outside. They shouldered their way through the door and crowded Bvekenya against the wall. "You Bvekenya?" asked one.

"Yes."

"Then stick your hands up. Any nonsense and you'll get a bullet."

Both policemen had revolvers in their hands. Bvekenya was thunderstruck. He held his hands up and did some hard thinking.

"You're on the wrong side of the border aren't you?"

"So what?"

One of the policemen jammed his revolver into Bvekenya's ribs. The other pulled his hands down behind his back and slipped on a pair of handcuffs.

"You got a mule or horse?"

Bvekeyna nodded.

"Then get it saddled and collect your clobber. You're coming for a ride. Kiss your pal goodbye. He'll be a lot older before you meet again."

They kicked him outside. One of them gave him a clout in his face.

"By Gosh, Bvekenya, you've given us the slip so often it's a pleasure to have you in irons, even if we had to jump the border to do it."

They took Bvekenya to his camp. One of them bundled up his clothes and saw that Yapie the mule was caught and saddled. Then they put Bvekenya in the saddle. They tied the links of his handcuffs to the back of his saddle, collected their own mules and set off for the north, with six African constables keeping them company.

It was a two weeks' ride through the bush. Relations were hardly cordial. Social contact was confined to an occasional curse. The policemen proferred no charge and Bvekenya made no attempt to escape.

They arrived at the Rhodesian administrative centre of Fort Victoria, and Bvekenya tried the comforts of its gaol. There was still no charge. After a few days he started to protest so noisily that he was offered bail. He had no money on him, but he was a celebrated character in those parts. A local trader came, deposited £100 as bond, and offered him hospitality until the trial.

Days passed. The police watched him closely. They were obviously trying to drum up evidence. There were enough possible charges against Bvekenya, but the problem was to get witnesses. The tribespeople only looked at the police blankly when the question of evidence was raised. They had to live with Bvekenya as a tough neighbour in the bush, and getting him a few years in gaol was not likely to make their old age comfortable.

Eventually a couple of Shanganes were induced to swear that they had seen Bvekenya shoot a hippo. Compared to the other possibilities, the charge was laughable. He was fined £5. His host and a second trader paid the fine. That was all. His host lent him some money and he bought a new 9.7 rifle from one of the local policemen. Then he set out for home, shooting seven elephants and recruiting several dozen Rhodesian tribesmen as he travelled, to compensate him for his trouble.

He wondered what lay behind the arrest. The police were obviously making an effort to clean up the illegal recruiters, although they were hardly successful. Only a few of the amateurs had been caught. Fred Roux had been arrested and fined £50, although he was not even recruiting. But since he was an amateur it was easier to get the Africans to trump up evidence against him. Even the Portuguese were more active, with their police raiding through the bush; but, so far as Bvekenya was concerned, always taking care to raid one of his camps the day after he had left.

It was only when Bvekenya returned to Makhuleke that he discovered the reason for the enterprise of the police. On the heights of the Lubombo range, just across the Pafuri River from his camp at Crooks Corner, there were signs and sounds of activity. The official recruiting organisation of the mines was busy constructing a depot.

Bvekenya walked over through the bush on a visit. His appearance created so much embarrassment he guessed immediately the reason for his arrest. The mines had put great pressure on the police to rid the bush of the blackbirders, for they wanted to establish their own organisation.

Paul Neergaard, who was in charge of the camp, was obviously scared of being shot. Working for his organisation was one thing, but dying for it was another. He swallowed hard and had a long talk with Bvekenya.

"It's no good trying to fight big money on your own," he said, "unless you're going to have a bloody revolution. Why don't you go up to Johannesburg and talk it over with the big boys? If they think they can make money out of you they'll soon forget your past."

Bvekenya was inclined to agree. A visit to civilisation would certainly do him no harm. Besides, he had found a message waiting for him at Makhuleke to the effect that his sister Trixie, married to a farmer named William Green, was dying; and he would like to see her. Accordingly, he packed up and went off to Johannesburg.

He arrived in the city the day after his sister's funeral. It was quite a blow. He had not seen any member of his own family for fourteen years; and to meet them all again, still gathered together in the sadness following a funeral, was miserable.

He discussed affairs with them. William Green was in a particularly unhappy state. He and Trixie had been living with their family on a farm called Vlakplaas in the western Transvaal, near the tiny centre of Geysdorp. Now he wanted to leave, raise some money to educate his children, and start afresh. Bvekenya helped him there. He bought the 557 morgen farm from his brother-in-law for £1700 cash and arranged that his old father would settle there and care for the place until Bvekenya eventually left the bush and wanted a home.

Then Bvekenya went up to see the mine magnates. In the person of their labour recruiting representative they were not as bad as he had expected.

"You could be valuable to us, Barnard," the representative said, looking at him curiously. "You must have made a small fortune from your activities. Don't you think it's time you settled down and came on the right side of the law? We'll let bygones be bygones. You go over to Pretoria and see the police. Get yourself cleared of anything sticky, and then join us as a recruiter. You can work in your old haunts under Neergaard at Pafuri. We'll give you £50 a month salary, with the prospect that if you make good you'll get a recruiting station of your own. How about it?"

Bvekenya thought it worth a try. He had a tidy sum saved by then, and a farm of his own to stock. Respectability suddenly had certain advantages. He nodded.

"I'll try it."

He went over to Pretoria the next day to see the police. He asked for the Commissioner and was shown to his deputy, a pleasant enough policeman, sitting drinking his tea. He rose as Bvekenya entered and shook hands affably.

"My name is S.C. Barnard," said Bvekenya. "I want to find out what crimes you have against me."

The policeman sat down.

"Well, Mr. Barnard, I can't recollect anything. I'll enquire, but why do you ask? I don't know of any Barnards in serious trouble. Where do you come from?"

"From Crooks Corner. You people know me as Bvekenya."

The policeman almost hit the ceiling.

"You, Bvekenya?"

He stared at Bvekenya in amazement, taking in all the details of the big, brawny, sunburned man before him.

"For over ten years we've been trying to get you, and now I find you in my office."

He leaned back in his chair and roared with laughter. After a while he stubbed his fingers into the bell buttons on his desk. Bvekenya expected a riot squad. Two constables came in.

"Bring some more tea, the files on Bvekenya, and ask the Commissioner if he'd mind calling this way. Tell him we have a celebrity visiting us today."

He stared at Bvekenya in wonder.

"If you only knew how many man hours we've wasted on you."

Bvekenya smiled. If the policeman only knew how many rumours had warned him that the border was alive with *maFokies* (detectives), *maJohnies* (white policemen) and *maPorika* (black policemen): all searching for him, while he lay snug in his camp on the Tshefu.

The Commissioner came in and seemed highly amused. More tea arrived, and a sizable folder. The two policemen browsed through it. From their faces, it must have made interesting reading.

"We certainly seem to have wanted you often, and badly," said the Commissioner. "But these charges grow stale, you know."

He looked at Bvekenya quizzically.

"Most of them seem to be assaults with intent and poaching complaints. They're all stale."

"What about this one," said his subordinate. "We have a complaint that you were seen smuggling eighty rifles and fifty cases of ammunition, carried on your two donkeys, over the Portuguese border. You cannot disturb our most ancient and gallant Portuguese ally, you know. We were asked to investigate the complaint by the government under the Defence of the Realm Act."

"Government should have asked you rather to buy my two donkeys," said Bvekenya.

"Why so?"

"For two donkeys to carry that weight? Ammunition, rifles, my food and my clothing, and then to outrun the police? They must have been elephants rather than donkeys. No, sir, I'm no gunrunner."

"Well, you have something there," said the Commissioner dubiously. "So far as we are concerned, apart from these old assaults with intent and a couple of poachings, there's nothing we want you for. The epicentre of your disturbances seems to have been on the Portuguese side of the frontier. From there your reputation has spread far and wide, and the further it's spread the worse it's become. Well, we can't arrest you for a reputation, although it certainly interests us. The assaults and the poaching are all too far back. We won't resurrect them. In any case, what do you propose doing now?"

Bvekenya told them. They approved.

"You can tell your employers that, so far as we are concerned, you have a clean slate. But what of the Portuguese? There's no clean slate there, you know. They want you for what looks like nearly every crime under the sun. I'd love to know for which one they most want you – assault, poaching, blackbirding, and a dozen or so more; which is it?"

Bvekenya smiled but said nothing. Deep within him he guessed what had riled the Portuguese most. When the floods were on and all communications disrupted, the Portuguese at Massangena, who were largely employed in hunting him, had run short of rations. They had sent a party of Africans tramping along to Makhuleke store for emergency supplies.

Bvekenya had met them and asked where they were going. When they told him their mission, he examined the list of requirements. Flour, canned meat, sugar, salt, tea and coffee: all were there, as well as an underlined item for one cask of pure olive oil.

"They won't understand this at the store," Bvekenya had told the bearers. He rubbed out the "Olive" and substituted "Castor". Several days later he saw the party homeward bound with the goods. Two of the bearers were laboriously carrying an enormous keg of pure castor oil.

"That'll certainly keep them busy if they use it for cooking,'" he thought with a laugh; and he had noticed an increased malevolence in the Portuguese raids ever afterwards.

Bvekenya went back to his new life at Pafuri with considerable interest. He was at his happiest roving around in the bush recruiting and hunting, and the risks and the danger always exhilarated him. He had no desire to abandon the life; but just how he would take to working for others remained to be seen.

Bvekenya had developed his own recruiting business to a high level; and this, in fact, was what the official organisation most wanted to take over. Bvekenya, therefore, showed them his paths, the most dependable drinking pools in the bush, the wells he had dug and the compounds he had erected in the bush. At most of the difficult river crossings he had also stationed canoes with ferrymen, while at the junction of the Limpopo and Pafuri rivers he had a proper boat, railed up from Durban to Pietersburg for him and then dragged down to Crooks Corner on a donkey wagon.

Bvekenya had improved the main ivory trail from Makhuleke to Mavombe and off to Louis Trichardt into a usable road. He had even brought several grain storage tanks along it, and a "Colonist" mill, which he floated down the Limpopo from Makhuleke for the eleven miles to the junction of the Pafuri where his main camp had stood, at the farthest point of Crooks Corner.

Selling the mill to the recruiting organisation was quite an event in the bush. Part of the sale agreement stated that he would dismantle the mill, carry it to a remote bush camp on the 22° latitude, and there re-erect it.

He dismantled the mill and loaded the parts onto the backs of a string of donkeys. The mill-wheel, a spoked metal affair, was placed on the back of Yapie the mule, giving that perky little animal quite a remarkable appearance.

They set off along the path to the new camp, with the donkeys strung out ahead and the mule dawdling along in the rear, snatching an occasional mouthful of grass here and there and then running to catch up. Bvekenya always left

Yapie largely to his own devices, for he was an independent animal, very stubborn if he thought he was being interfered with but a good worker if left alone.

At the head of the file of donkeys, Bvekenya rode into a Shangane village. There the headman promptly warned him that the Portuguese police were in the next village collecting taxes. Bvekenya rode on, but did a distinct detour around the village. Yapie had lagged behind, but he could normally be depended upon to follow the trail of his master ahead of him.

This time Yapie slipped up. With his mind on a mealie he had stolen in the village, he overshot the point where Bvekenya had led the donkeys out of the path. Suddenly awakening to the fact that he was lost, Yapie broke into a smart canter along the path. He was confused and felt horribly dismayed. He was an orderly sort of mule who panicked easily.

Feeling more and more abandoned, he promptly lost his head. He raced straight on at speed into the next village, braying for Bvekenya to wait for him. He tore into the village centre, with the mill-wheel bouncing on his back. He skidded past the astounded Portuguese, sitting at a table collecting taxes; scattered a line of Shanganes waiting to pay; and ran out into the bush again. Ever afterwards the Portuguese had the idea that Bvekenya carried artillery with him. The mill-wheel on Yapie and rumours of the file of donkeys laden with metal parts gave them many sleepless nights.

Yapie, by then, was getting old. From his encounters with lions at the camp on the Tshefu he also had a stiff hind leg, which gave him some trouble with the coming of age. Bvekenya liked the little mule and decided to pension him off. He had some old donkeys lazing about at Khombo's kraal near Makhuleke. There he pensioned off Yapie; but the mule's retirement, unfortunately, did not last long. One night a pride of lions sneaked across the Limpopo in the shallows, and poor Yapie was sausages by morning. Bvekenya was sorry to lose him.

Several other friends from the old days of Crooks Corner were also departing. The one and only William Pye went down with influenza in 1918. Bvekenya and Buchanan tried to nurse him. He was certainly a happy patient. Even though he knew he was dying, he was still laughing and cracking jokes. He died one evening while his women howled around the hut. They buried him next morning, close to Hartman's grave in the cemetery of Crooks Corner.

Most of the other blackbirders had abandoned Crooks Corner. With even Bvekenya turned honest, there was little chance for them. The place became quiet and almost deserted. At the store of Makhuleke business fell off, and even Buchanan decided it was time to leave. At the end of 1919 he packed his kit and left the place for a farm he had bought in the Soutpansberg.

Bvekenya was really making an effort to return to the ways of civilised men. His farm was well stocked by then. He had invested money in animals and tools; and each holiday his employers allowed him was spent on the place, preparing its ground and buildings, its sheds and paddocks, with the ultimate idea of retiring there.

There was, in those days, quite an extensive wood-cutting business in the fine timber around the kraal of Sikokololo (where Punda Milia stands today). Old Joseph Fourie was one of the many who cut timber there. One mahogany log he cut was famous. It filled his biggest wagon, and a double span of oxen had difficulty in moving it. Like all other heavy logs, it was loaded by using the wagon's screw jacks to raise the one end; then manoeuvring the wagon beneath it; locking the wheels; lowering the log; and then jacking up the further end of the trunk and sliding it into the wagon with the aid of the oxen.

Bvekenya cut the wood for most of his farmhouse furniture in this forest. He selected the magnificent wild mahogany trees to make his furniture, while his fence poles were cut from the termite-resistant *nsimbitsi* (ironwood) trees. He transported the wood all the 500 miles to his farm by donkey wagon, using fourteen donkeys to a span and doing three seven-mile treks a day, with the usual resting and grazing spells in between.

In the course of these journeys, Bvekenya first learned just how far his renown had spread. Every wagon-man he met seemed to have heard stories which invariably painted him in the blackest colours of murder and outrage. The Transvaal lowveld has always been a great manufactory of yarns. Perhaps it is the heat of the day and the mellowing effect of sundowners that stimulates imaginations to such fertility. At all events, most wonderful tales were spread abroad of the doings of the folk of Crooks Corner. Each odd character had as many tales woven around him as a tree standing in its autumn leaves; and the older the tales – like the leaves – the yellower, mellower, and more unrecognisable they had become.

Bvekenya had many surprises, listening to these tales of his remarkable deeds. The ultimate experience came when he was returning along the road between Rustenburg and Warmbad. At one watering place he found a strange wagon outspanned by the roadside. After he had released his donkeys to graze Bvekenya strolled over to greet the wagon-man. The stranger was not a very prepossessing-looking individual but he seemed affable enough.

"Hullo," he said, holding out his hand, "I'm Barnard."

"That's odd," said Bvekenya, shaking his hand. "I'm also a Barnard."

"Ah," said the man, "but I'm a famous Barnard. I'm Bvekenya, the poacher."

He proceeded to tell some choice tales illustrating his prowess and bravado. Bvekenya listened with interest. When the man stopped for breath Bvekenya could not resist the chance.

"Well, they're interesting tales," he said, "but it's strange I've never heard them before. You're a bit mistaken in your identity brother, I'm that Barnard and you're a liar."

The other Barnard gulped and withdrew hurriedly.

"My donkeys are straying," he said. "I'll be back and we can sort this out."

Bvekenya waited, but his rival returned no more. The only sound of him was the noise of his wagon rolling away through the bush. Imitation, it is said, is the sincerest form of flattery; but Bvekenya was irked. If the public wanted to believe all the nonsense told about him, there was nothing he could do about it. But if they thought he resembled the scabby little runt who had sought to impersonate him, then his vanity was grievously wounded.

If Bvekenya's visits to the outside world produced novelties for him, then their effect on his Shangane hunters was paralysing. Bvekenya once stopped at De Fon Siku's hotel at Klein Letaba. He had two young Shanganes with him carrying his belongings, including some food for the road: a great, fat breast of eland and a big, greasy, black tin of mealie porridge.

Bvekenya was in the bar when the lunch gong went. The two young Shanganes were sitting in the shade behind the hotel. They had never before heard a gong.

"What is it?" they asked the hotel servants.

"It is the sound that the white men want their food," somebody told them.

The Shanganes looked at each other and shrugged. The ways of white people were odd, but if that was what the sound meant they knew what to do.

"Where is our master?" they asked.

"There, in that room on the side, with the tables."

They pushed through the swing doors and trooped self-consciously through the diners to Bvekenya's table. On top of it they dumped the breast of eland and the greasy can of porridge. By the time they had been ejected the Portuguese proprietor was almost having a stroke.

Bvekenya often felt himself out of place and uncomfortable in the world of civilisation, law and order. He and the recruiting organisation were strange bedfellows. Bvekenya, to tell the truth, was not cut out by the fates to be a model employee. He was too much of an individualist to flourish in the body of an organisation as autocratic as the mining business and its labour-recruiting satellite.

By 1923 relations were becoming somewhat strained. He thought about his future with concern. The prospect of remaining a dutiful servant to a succession of chiefs whose promotion came from their education or influence rather than their experience, was not particularly attractive. Blackbirding may have been ended, but the elephants were still there and ivory remained valuable. He decided to cut himself adrift once more and go back to the bush. He had no qualms or regrets. By the end of the year he was off after elephants. Once again his gun was his best friend and most constant companion, and a thousand miles of wilderness his home and safe refuge.

SEVENTEEN

The bushrangers

In the years that followed his return to the bush, Bvekenya hunted with success and delight. Compared to the tyro who had first entered the bush in 1910 with a decrepit .303 as his principal weapon, the Bvekenya of the late 1920s was a highly experienced hunter, generally recognised as the king of all poachers in Southern Africa.

With his experience his taste in guns had matured, until he selected his armament with the fastidiousness of a connoisseur.

When shooting elephants one is always caught in an awkward predicament. A big gun will kill with ease, but the noise alarms every elephant within miles. A small gun only kills with difficulty and the exercise of considerable skill; but, in compensation, the sharp whip-crack noise it makes is so like the sound of an elephant pushing down a tree that no animal takes alarm.

After his second gun, a 9.5 whose short barrel made it convenient but prescribed much drive, Bvekenya tried a 4.25 Magnum Express, a magazine rifle but somewhat disappointing.

Then he bought a 4.65 double-barrelled Magnum Express, made by Holland & Holland in London. This was the heaviest and best gun Bvekenya ever used, and he shot many elephants with it. Once he nursed the project of having a bigger gun made to his own specifications. He went so far as to send an order to the Mannlicher-Schönauer factory for a 15 mm magazine rifle. With this weapon he reckoned he would get in a triangular shot: the elephant would go one way, the gun another, and Bvekenya the third way; but there would be no argument as to what had happened to the elephant.

The factory replied to his order with a cable.

"Such a gun impossible. Who wants to fire it, giant or madman?"

Bvekenya, accordingly, stuck to his 4.65. With this weapon his favourite shot was from the animal's side, behind the shoulder, into the heart and lungs. Behind the eyes, from the side, was also a good shot, but a much smaller target at which to aim.

From the rear, if it were impossible to get a side shot, he would aim at the backbone just above the tail. This would pull the animal down and allow time for one of the fatal side shots.

Trying to shoot an elephant from the front was a fool's venture at best; but if necessity forced his hand in a charge Bvekenya would shoot between the eyes, not with the hope of killing the animal, but rather with the hope of turning him.

The ability to find a target without any time lag was Bvekenya's greatest professional asset. With mental alertness, a first-class rifle which he always carried himself, and tremendous stamina to stand the strain of an arduous life, he had all the qualities necessary for success in his chosen occupation, providing Providence did not blot him out with that summary ending which has been the lot of many professional hunters.

When Bvekenya returned to the bush there were very few of the old professional hunters still left. Times were changing; and civilisation, with its advance guard of the policeman and the game warden, was gradually making the life of the bushranger too precarious for either comfort or profit.

Fred Roux and Monty Ash were about the only other two hunters operating on the Portuguese side of the frontier, and even their visits were becoming erratic. The Portuguese and Rhodesian authorities were making it more risky to poach game, and the Transvaal police were making it difficult to smuggle the tusks and whips back to any profitable market. As a final difficulty, the Kruger National Park was being properly organised and a ranger's post had recently been established at the site of old Sikokololo's kraal. Admittedly, the pioneer ranger at what was first called *Punda Maria*, Captain *"Ou Kat"* Coetser, was more of a poacher himself than a conservationist; but he was obviously the thin end of the wedge, leading towards the ultimate strict enforcement of the law in the old no-man's-land of Crooks Corner.

Bvekenya had several narrow escapes from being caught red-handed in his poaching. One day he shot an elephant in Rhodesia. It fell dead, very inconsiderately, right next to a main path. The local tribespeople warned Bvekenya that they expected a police patrol to pass that way next morning, and the sight of the carcass would certainly warn them that some poacher was operating in their territory. Complications could be awkward for the tribespeople and Bvekenya.

The carcass could not be moved. The only way out was to make a new path. The headman drummed up assistance from neighbouring kraals, and all night long the people worked. They planted trees and grass carefully along the old path. Meanwhile, long files of women tramped the newly-made detour around the carcass until the ground was firm and hard. As much meat as possible was also cut from the carcass overnight and scattered in the bush miles away, so that the vultures would be decoyed into dispersing far from the dead elephant.

The Rhodesian police were generally becoming embarrassing to a hard-working poacher. Bvekenya was spending some months there shooting hippos for sjamboks when a police patrol again came into his vicinity at an awkward time. He had just shot two hippos, and they had floated to the surface of a pool. News came that the patrol was approaching and could be expected to spend the night camped by the banks of the pool.

This time, fortunately, it was easy to conceal the carcasses. The floating hippos were hastily cut open, the internal gasses released, and a few buckets of sand and rocks poured into them. Grass ropes were tied to their legs and they were then allowed to sink. The police came as expected, spent a comfortable night in their camp, and then moved on. Next day the tribespeople dragged the carcasses out and life went on as before.

Monty Ash also had some close shaves with the authorities at this time. Pursuing two elephants once, he found the animals drawing too close to a Portuguese administrative post. He sent a couple of his Shanganes to the Portuguese with the news that if they came quickly they could catch Monty Ash. The Portuguese set off with their guides and were led a safe twenty miles in the opposite direction. Ash, meanwhile, pursued the elephants. He actually ran them down in the garden of the administrative post. He shot them, removed the tusks and vanished into the bush, leaving the carcasses for the Portuguese to find when they came tramping back after their guides had given them the slip.

Bvekenya never resorted to any stratagem quite so spectacular, but once he did shoot an elephant so close to a police post that it was inevitable somebody would find the carcass and start a hue and cry. As it happened, he had found an elephant dead recently, with tusks so undersized that he had taken them more for their value as curiosities than anything else. He extracted the tusks of the elephant he had shot. Then he enlarged the bullet wound until it looked as though a tusk might have done the fatal damage. He then told the local tribesmen to take the undersized tusks to the policemen, tell them of the carcass, and explain that the elephant had died in a fight with another of its own kind, and that these were the tusks, so small that the animal had been unable to defend itself.

These stratagems were all ingenious, but it was symptomatic of changing conditions in the bush that the poachers were forced to resort to them at all. In the old days the bush was inviolate as a fortress against police or official intervention; and in his years of wandering Bvekenya had encountered some strange characters who had found sanctuary there.

In the early days, around 1912, one curious individual wandered into the bush from the Transvaal. He had a flock of big Boer goats with him and he had trained some of these animals to carry small pack saddles with his goods and bedding. He wandered about in the bush for years with his goats: milking them, killing one occasionally for food, and protecting the herd from the constant attack of lions and hyenas. Eventually the goat-man vanished. What happened to him is unknown; but his goats, and their descendants, are still to be found scattered among the kraals of the Shanganes and at the Portuguese administrative posts.

Even stranger than the goat-man were the three De Beer brothers: Herclaas, Theunis and Jan. This odd trio migrated from the Waterberg to the Melsetter district in Rhodesia in 1892. One morning in 1896 they went out shooting. They shot a rietbok and collected some honey. They dined so well that night and liked the free and easy hunting life so well that they did not even bother to return home to collect their belongings. They simply wandered on and on into the wilds and returned to civilisation no more.

Their boots gave in, their clothes were torn to rags, and they were soon reduced to loincloths and head scarves. They became proper wild men of the woods with no personal impedimenta, blankets or equipment. The only comfort they had was a fire at night; and around it they would huddle like three great, longhaired, shaggy dogs, in search of warmth.

The De Beers consumed food as though they were a triple-mouthed mincing machine. They ate anything: game, birds, insects or reptiles were all equally palatable to them. The big, fat wood-borer (*mabungu*) grubs were their particular delight, while odd little creatures such as the tiny elephant shrews were caught in traps and served as relish.

If they bagged some larger animal they would camp around its carcass. They would obtain a supply of drinking water in calabashes and then settle down to feed. They would eat and eat: grilling, roasting and frying; crunching bones, scraping out marrow; falling down gorged; sleeping; struggling up, and eating again until the animal was totally consumed. The three of them could eat a giraffe down to its hooves in three days, and then end up hungry. They never kept any food in reserve. They would simply starve until they shot or trapped something else.

Their idea of a menu was often curious. Bvekenya met them once. They had just shot an eland and they asked him to dine with them. They made it a special occasion in his honour. There were tortoises and lizards. Then they served what they called "veld curry". Bvekenya tucked into the mess and found it good. He asked what it was. It was the eland's stomach, cut up and boiled with all its contents.

The De Beers were very shy of other Europeans. Once they visited Ballantyne's store at Mount Selinda in Rhodesia. Ballantyne was himself a curious character. He was a canny old Scots bachelor. His store was doing a roaring trade, but he never spent a penny. He ate out of the lid of a pot to save buying a plate. He boiled up his tea leaves until the drink was almost pure water, and he had never been known to have his bedroom swept out. The floor was three inches deep in used matches.

Ballantyne found the De Beers sitting on the veranda of his store, among the Africans. Despite his care with money, he was a kindly man. He took pity on the three scarecrows before him.

"Wait until the rush is over," he said, "then I'll fix you up."

Ballantyne intended to give the bushrangers some new clothes, but they failed to understand this. The "fix up" sounded ominous. It might mean anything from a thrashing to a forcible bath. The De Beers bolted and were seen no more at Mount Selinda.

Despite their wildness, the De Beers were a kind-hearted and honest trio. Bvekenya found it profitable to employ them as touts and recruiters in his blackbirding business. They worked for him until 1914. Then Jan died of sun-stroke, while another bushranger named Barend Bezuidenhout, who had joined forces with them, died of fever. These deaths, together with rumours of the war, upset the two surviving brothers.

They decided to leave the bush. Bvekenya paid them their accumulated commission. It amounted to £994, in sovereigns. The amount of money awed them. They took daily turns to carry the gold. Every night they would empty the sack out onto a blanket and count the money, quarrelling madly if they miscounted and found anything short.

They intended to go farming. On their way out along the ivory trail they bought some cows and a bull from Monty Ash. These animals were to be the first livestock on their farm – but their hunger for meat was a mania. The first night along the road they killed the bull, and camped until they had eaten it. The whole road was milestoned with the bones of similar feasts. By the time they reached their farm, all the animals had been eaten.

The farm was on the Sand River, near Pietersburg. They stocked it up with cattle, but their appetite was their ruin. They ate all their animals and gradually changed their savings into meat. They would send pack mules to the nearest butcher and buy enormous hunks of beef. Eventually the butcher took their farm to settle his account. They never returned to the bush. Conditions were getting too difficult in the wilds and they were not adventurers, although they were certainly the roughest of all the bushrangers. Herclaas eventually died in a fall of gravel on the diamond diggings.

There was another strange character whose appearance in the wilds was of purely a transitory nature. This bird of passage was seen tramping along the Sofala path, with a donkey carrying his few belongings and a sack of money.

His story was ingenious. The railway from Pietersburg to Louis Trichardt was about to be built. There was much competition and argument among the farmers about the precise location of the line. Everybody wanted the line to pass their own property, so that ground values would boom and their farms could enjoy the advantages of a siding.

Into this fertile ground of intrigue, string-pulling and speculation, appeared a surveyor with theodolite and detailed maps. He was to locate the line. He immediately became a popular figure. Hospitality was lavished upon him. Every farmer vied with his neighbour in entertaining the surveyor.

They stood him drinks. He could work his will with food, property and women.

Individuals and syndicates approached him privately with lucrative offers. Money changed hands. By the time the surveyor had accommodated all his friends the railway plan must have looked as complicated as a monkey rope, so much did it twist, turn and double in its tracks in order to serve everyone with sidings and stations.

At the end of his survey the surveyor took to the Sofala path. It twisted, but never so much as his imaginary railway line, for he had never had anything officially to do with it at all. From Sofala he sailed to parts unknown, and Southern Africa knew him no more.

Some of the bushrangers proper also found Sofala a convenient backdoor through which to slip when their lives became precarious. Thomas Adams was one of the several who found that a quick exit from Africa was very desirable.

This Thomas Adams was an odd individual, thought by some to be the notorious Thomas Polus, who kept the frontier areas in disturbance prior to the Anglo-Boer War.

In 1910 this individual, whoever he was, was recruiting along the Great Save River in company with a New Zealander named Powdrell who ran a store in Rhodesia. Adams acted as Powdrell's recruiter and hunter; and the trader had come down to settle up with his employee.

Five miles up the river, another recruiter by the name of Leonard Henry Ledeboer had his camp. Ledeboer was a Hollander who had first come to South Africa back in 1888 and served his apprenticeship in the bush with such renowned experts as Selous.

One evening, when Ledeboer was sitting at his fire and the mists hung over the great river like ghosts, a man suddenly walked out of the darkness. It was Adams. He sat down and told his story. He and Powdrell had gone hunting for wild geese that afternoon. Powdrell had shot a bird and waded through the reeds to recover it. A crocodile had waylaid him. He had been carried off, and now Adams was on his way to report to the police. He was in such a hurry that he refused to rest for longer than a drink and smoke before he went on into the bush and the night.

Ledeboer thought the story over. At dawn he walked down to Powdrell's camp. He asked the Shanganes there what had happened. Adams' story sounded good to Ledeboer, but the man had neglected to tell it to the Shanganes. They said Powdrell had been murdered.

With Ledeboer, the Shanganes set out to find the body. Ledeboer walked along the riverbanks, while the Shanganes paddled through the reeds in a canoe. Half a mile down the river they found the site of the crime: the bloodstains and the place where a body had been dragged through the reeds to the water. They probed about in the water with poles. Soon they found the body, with its head shot in. A money belt, which had contained about £200 for bribing chiefs and paying wages, was missing.

Ledeboer buried the body and reported to the police, but Adams had got well away. He went to the kraal he had rescued from the man-eating lions some time before. The villagers hid and fed him, for they had a debt of gratitude. Then they guided him safely to Sofala, and in this manner he escaped completely.

One of the few bushrangers who used Sofala as an entrance rather than an exit for his activities was the well-known Charlie Diegel. Diegel, a tall, fair-haired man with a light ginger beard, was born in Cassell, in Germany. He slipped across the frontier into Holland in order to avoid army service, and then found his way to Sofala. At that half-forgotten little port, he set up in business as a fisherman and seller of dried fish.

Then Diegel removed into the bush. He met Lambert and went into partnership with him until that individual vanished. Then Diegel linked up with another bushranger, a Swiss named Zeefliet who eventually died of blackwater fever at the junction of the Save and Lundi rivers. Diegel promptly found a third partner, in the shape of a Greek named Considine; and for some little while worked in harmony with this individual, recruiting and hunting.

Diegel was particularly renowned for his whips and sjamboks. While Considine recruited, Diegel hunted in order to provide food for the recruits and leather for the whips. Considine took a gang of recruits down to Crooks Corner once and left Diegel on the Save River, shooting hippos and making sjamboks. The Greek considered that he needed a holiday. He had a hut in Crooks Corner, and to this retreat he withdrew with the proceeds from the last gang of recruits.

Some weeks of hard drinking followed. Diegel, meanwhile, worked on with his sjamboks until his supplies ran low. Then he sent two of his Shanganes in with a string of donkeys, laden with sjamboks and a letter for Considine, complaining that all the food left was venison and salt. If Considine was not coming back himself soon, could he please send some food with the Shanganes?

Considine had a curious sense of humour. He gave the Shanganes a bag of salt and told them to take it to their master. Diegel failed to see the joke. A furious row broke out between the partners, argued at long distance by means of threats and abuse. For months the two men behaved like a couple of dogs snarling at each other through a fence; threatening dire consequences if only they could get at each other, although both well knew that the gate beside them was standing wide open.

Bvekenya watched proceedings with interest. He often met one or other of the men in the bush, and was regaled with stories of what they planned to do to each other. Occasionally he went so far as to direct them towards each other; but somehow or other they always managed to miss.

Once Bvekenya was travelling with Diegel when he noticed Considine's trail on the path. The trail was fresh and the chance too good to miss. Without telling Diegel, he led the way along the trail. Suddenly they turned a corner and came on Considine, camped beneath a tree. His dogs rushed out barking.

Considine crawled out from his shelter. He and Diegel stared at each other and then made a rush. It was one of those fights which start with promise but never get anywhere. Bvekenya felt as disappointed as a referee forced to disqualify two boxers for not fighting.

He separated the two men. They sat down to think their quarrel out. Suddenly Considine snatched up his gun and aimed it at Bvekenya.

"Blast you for bringing this German pig here," he said. "I am going to kill you for it."

Bvekenya took him at his word. He was sitting on a tree trunk. He put his foot against the trunk and dived at Considine's stomach. The Greek went flying, his gun in one direction, his wind in another. Bvekenya sprawled on top of him. He lifted the man and tied him up in the good old fashion of his culture of the bush. Then they did some hard talking.

There was little to be gained in starting a feud. They agreed to separate. Considine wandered off to Rhodesia, where the police soon arrested him for illegal recruiting. After a spell in gaol he made his way back to Portuguese territory. On the journey he died of blackwater fever. His Shanganes loaded his body on a mule, plugged their nostrils, and took him all the way down to Makhuleke. They were frightened of simply burying him in the bush, for fear they might be accused of his murder. He was buried in the cemetery of Crooks Corner.

Diegel went on with his hunting. He was a curious soul and not much of a shot. There is a story of how he was once in much reduced circumstances. He usually wandered around with a Shangane attendant, a pack loaded with his goods and a plentiful supply of Worcester sauce, Diegel being uncommonly partial to that condiment with his venison.

At the time of this story (1912) he was reduced to just his Shangane, carrying a calabash of drinking water. He had shot nothing for days. Then fortune favoured him. South of the Great Save River he stumbled on the carcass of an elephant. The animal had been shot by a Shangane hunter named Mawube. The Shangane had concealed the carcass beneath mupani branches and then gone off to fetch his people for the feast.

Diegel decided with glee to make the elephant his own. He sent his attendant off on a twenty-mile walk to fetch more drinking water. The Shangane trudged off, leaving the usual trail of snapped twigs so that he could find his way back.

Diegel, meanwhile, made his camp beside the elephant and began to cut up the carcass. He immediately found that the elephant's stomach was full of water. The animal had apparently drunk the usual prodigious quantity only a short while before being shot.

This discovery of water was the ultimate to Diegel's stroke of luck. He knew how to purify water. The bowels containing the water he bound up with grass. Then he emptied one bowel, rinsed it with water, tied up one end and filled it with sand.

He suspended this bowel from a tree, with the open end upwards. Then he pricked a few holes in the bottom end. The water-laden bowel was dragged up the tree and matters were so contrived that the water would drip into the sand-filled bowel.

He then cut off one of the elephant's ears. This was turned into a great dish, lying on the ground to catch the water as it filtered through the sand. The filtration plant soon began to work. Then thousands of thirsty insects arrived for a drink. Diegel had to take off his shirt and arrange it into a shelter over the elephant's ear, in order to protect the water.

With his water supply problem solved, Diegel began to cut out fat, for this part of an elephant was of vital importance to him in sjambok making. He cut an entrance into the elephant's stomach. He took off his remaining clothes and climbed right inside, emerging every now and then with the best pieces of fat and suspending them on the trees.

While thus engaged, Mawube and his people arrived, carrying big pots slung on poles to fill with meat. Diegel was inside the elephant at the time, and his hearing was never good.

The Shanganes saw the chunks of fat and the entrails suspended in the trees. Mawube was outraged.

"Who has the right to cut out my fat?" he wailed.

The noise penetrated to Diegel. He stirred in the depths of the animal's stomach and clambered out of the entrance: a long, white slab of a man, with his matted yellow hair down to his shoulders and his whole person caked in blood.

There was a long moment of silence. This was the apparition to end all apparitions. There was a thud as somebody dropped a pot. Then a wild shout and a crashing through the bush as the Shanganes headed for the horizon. Diegel was left to the carcass in peace.

Diegel always cut the tips off his bullets, so that they would make a bigger hole and prove more certainly fatal. This was practical with small animals, but with big game it could be disastrous.

The First World War had broken out, when Bvekenya received a message to say that Diegel had been injured. He had tried to shoot a buffalo with his soft-pointed bullets. The shot had failed to kill. The animal had chased him through the bush and crushed him against a baobab tree. For some reason, the animal had then left him; he was badly hurt.

It was an awkward time for Bvekenya. His brother-in-law, Billy Green, had come into the bush to join him and was down with blackwater fever. Bvekenya rode all through the night to reach Diegel. He made a rough hammock and tried to carry him; but the pain from the jolting was too great. All Bvekenya could do was make him comfortable and then return to Billy Green.

He carried Billy Green a few miles nearer, until he had the two patients about fifteen miles apart. Then he could just manage to attend to both of them each day. He did his best to aid them. For malaria or blackwater, Bvekenya always laid his patients down and washed them with water. He used a wet cloth, constantly wiping them and changing the water, until their temperatures went down. He had a theory that the cloth and the cool rubbing took the fever out. As soon as their temperatures dropped, he covered the patients up.

In Diegel's case, Bvekenya kept a cold poultice over the wounded stomach, just below the ribs where the buffalo had crushed him.

Food ran out. It was raining and the rivers were in flood. The Shanganes could not find any fording places through which to carry supplies. Bvekenya was forced to leave his patients and tramp off himself, to make a boat and fetch supplies from Makhuleke.

Fortunately both patients were getting better. While Bvekenya was away, however, the Portuguese police heard the story of Diegel's mishap from the Shanganes. They made the most of the chance. They wanted Diegel. They had several charges against him; and also he was a German, due for internment during the war. They raided through the bush and arrested the man. They slung a hammock on poles and carried him off.

When Bvekenya returned, he tried to chase the raiders; but they had three days' start. Diegel ended in the fort at Luanda in Angola, where some say he died in chains; but others have a rumour that he escaped to South West Africa. Billy Green recovered from his blackwater fever and went off safely home. In the end, only Bvekenya, of all the strange company he had once known, was left in the bush; and he well knew that his own days were numbered.

EIGHTEEN
Taller than the trees

The leaves of the tree of his life in the bush were falling, that Bvekenya knew; and yet there was much which he longed to achieve. There was the matter of Folage, the policeboy who had beaten him up – he still yearned for vengeance – and there was the matter of Dhlulamithi, the greatest of all elephants, who still roamed through the bush unchecked.

Of hunting Bvekenya had little to complain. The three hundred elephants the witch had promised him so many years ago had long since turned to bone and dust; and their ivory had brought him a comfortable profit. Hippos and antelope without number had fallen before his rifle. Their venison had provided him with many a feast, and their skins were scattered all over Southern Africa in the form of sjamboks and boot leather.

He continued to hunt with his habitual skill and fortune; but if the truth be told, Bvekenya was growing weary, and a trifle uneasy about his restless and destructive way of life.

He often thought both of his future and his past. The first thrill of hunting had long since gone. He had never found great delight in slaughtering any animal. He shot for profit, and the quicker his rifle brought death to his quarry the more he was pleased.

He had no illusions about himself or his fellows in the bush. From the very beginning, mankind has been a parasite on the sunburned back of Africa. The Bushmen, the Negro and the Bantu killed everything on sight, whether it was animal or lizard. The Dutch Voortrekkers and the host of British gold diggers and hunters passed over the country like a swarm of locusts: shooting, cutting down trees and destroying. Of them all, not one single racial group ever tried to understand or love Africa for herself. Instead, they were a curse to a land most generously endowed by Providence with a rich inheritance of animal life, timber, wild fruits and vegetables.

It often amazed Bvekenya when he heard of meat shortages in the cities of Southern Africa. Africa has traditionally been the home of vast herds of game. The South African has always claimed a deep love of biltong and venison; and yet not one single individual of all the multitude who had come to Africa ever attempted to conserve, breed and market the natural product of the land. Only the results of destruction had ever found their way to the markets.

Settlers had come and lavished skill, energy and fortune in cutting down natural timber and remarkable indigenous fruits which they viewed as weeds. Instead, they had planted imported trees and plants, and grazed exotic animals in place of the fat antelope they had slaughtered with wanton stupidity. Then they had cursed Africa and spent a fortune on scientific research, to find out why its peculiar environment had produced so many pests and ailments to destroy their exotic stock and crops.

Of all men, Bvekenya had the best chance to sample the rich variety of food in Africa. Of its meats, he had found the bush-pig to be fine, lean pork, naturally tough from its rugged life in the bush but always juicy. Its cousin the warthog was not as tasty, but it was also unmistakably pork.

Giraffe he had found pleasant-tasting, with a flavour somewhere between beef and mutton. Hippos were fat and extremely juicy and tender. Impala was so like mutton you could not tell the difference if it was served on an hotel table. Porcupine was very tender and good. Antbears had a curious flavour, probably because of their specialised diet; while zebra and waterbuck were the poorest of all game to eat: the waterbuck being dry and the zebra possessing a curious odour. The game birds, of course – the guineafowls, partridges and pheasants – were all delicious.

But the finest of all African antelope was without doubt the eland. Its meat was tender and magnificently flavoured, midway between beef and mutton. A big eland has as much meat on it as a large ox. No less than 40% of its live weight is pure meat, compared to the 30% on a domestic cow and 20% on a buffalo.

The eland is also a remarkably gentle animal. It is easily tamed and extremely docile to handle. It breeds with facility. It resists all African diseases and parasites; even the tsetse is impotent before it. Above all, it conserves rather than destroys the veld and the bush, for the bush is its natural home: it causes none of the erosion of goats and cattle and its water requirements are slight.

To Bvekenya it seemed that God in his kindness had given the eland to Africa; but man had destroyed and spurned it. Like a senseless jackal in a sheep-run, trigger-happy man had killed and butchered with an infantile pleasure and claimed to be enjoying good sport.

For years Bvekenya kept eland in his camp, and they wandered through the bush with him, as tame as a herd of cows. They are very easy to catch. He had trained all his dogs, such as Mac and Brits, to round up eland. The calves are born in June and July, and any dog trained to round up cattle has no difficulty in obtaining them, for the herds are not vicious. They kick sometimes but seldom poke, and even when wild are as easy to handle as cattle.

Each year Bvekenya caught a few calves. He would ride the animals down until they tired. Then his dogs would jump on them as soon as they fell, and keep them down without biting them. The calves seldom struggled. Bvekenya would tie them up very close to the trunk of a smooth tree, with no slack in their leads to allow them to injure themselves by jerking. He would give them water to drink from a bottle, and then two Shanganes would carry them to camp in a hammock.

They were tamed without any difficulty. He fed them cow's milk from a bottle, and tied them to a calf or another tame eland, so that they went to graze and drink together. In this way he had a herd of twelve eland roaming freely around his camp, and their rich and creamy milk never failed him for his coffee or tea.

He tried to interest others in the eland. He sent two of the animals to Forrestal in Rhodesia, but the Administrator responded with a fresh warrant for his arrest on a charge of trapping royal game. He tried to send some eland to his farm, but the Transvaal authorities prohibited their entry. Eventually he released them at Klopperfontein in the Kruger National Park, and their offspring are seen by many thousands of today's tourists.

Bvekenya experimented with other animals besides the eland. Buffalo he found to be magnificent trek oxen for wagons. They broke in well and were easily tamed, although the first generation remained somewhat irritable. They provided excellent milk as well as good beef and had a great capacity for work.

He even tried taming nyala, and once took a young doe he had found in a Shangane trap all the way to the Pretoria zoo as a gift, in the hope of interesting others in his projects.

Impala were also easy to tame, quite practical to handle, and their meat as tender as the finest mutton.

Catching the young animals occasionally provided some excitement. He saw a young zebra once and decided to add it to his domestic experiments. He gave his gun to one of his Shanganes and mounted his horse. He had a lively little chestnut Arab mare named Baba at that time. She was an experienced shooting horse and was obviously confused over Bvekenya's intentions.

She would race up to within ten yards of the zebra and then stop dead to allow Bvekenya to shoot. He would curse and spur the horse on, but Baba would always stop again when she reached what she evidently thought to be comfortable shooting range. At last Bvekenya resorted to the stratagem of throwing a thong at the zebra whenever the horse stopped. As this was the way she was always caught herself, Baba soon realised his intentions. She raced right up to the zebra.

Bvekenya wanted to drive the little animal into a clearing in the bush. He leaned down and caught hold of the zebra's ear. As he did so there was a vicious snarl. A lioness sprang up from the grass. She had been stalking an eland and Bvekenya had unwittingly driven the zebra right over her.

The lioness sprang at the zebra's head. Her teeth closed with a snap and took a lump out of Bvekenya's hand. Lioness, zebra, horse and Bvekenya tumbled over in a heap. It was quite a surprise for all concerned. Baba scrambled up and raced for the bush. The lioness sat down next to the zebra and started to growl uncertainly.

Bvekenya had no weapon of any description. He tried to frighten the lioness by clapping his hands and shouting, but for an hour she sat there and growled at him. She was too frightened to charge him, and he was too cautious to move. They sat and faced each other over the stricken zebra, and it was a long hour.

Then the lioness stood up. She turned tail and wandered disconsolately away. Bvekenya returned to camp. Only the unfortunate zebra remained to mark the site of the unexpected climax to the chase. Next morning the Shanganes went and buried the little animal in their capacious stomachs, and there was an end to the matter.

It was not only the idea of farming game which attracted Bvekenya; the wild fruits of Africa seemed to him to be potentially profitable commercially. There were fruits of delicious flavour growing wild in the bush, and he well knew the fortune that awaited any man who introduced the public of the world to these new flavours in jams and drinks.

There was *makwakwa*, the wild orange, with its delightful scent. Each year the Shanganes collected the fruit and dried it. The skin was the part they particularly relished. They ground it up and stored it for the winter. It has a flavour like slightly bitter dates, and is an excellent vegetable with meat.

Then there was *ntinzinde*, the wild plum, black in colour, and a sweet, juicy fruit to the taste.

Masala, the small, round pumpkin-like fruit, with a sweet smell and a pleasant flavour, was another natural product of the bush. The *nja*, like a brown coloured date pip, was a favourite of the elephant and African alike, while innumerable other fruits made life in the wilds pleasant at their time of ripening.

There were remarkable wild vegetables as well, both attractive to the taste and full of nutritious vitamins.

There is the wild sweet potato (*magurri*) which the Shangane women use so much. The wild chicory tree (*shukutzu*) yields a brittle root which when dried, ground and roasted, provided Bvekenya with coffee.

Gwangwate, the bulrush, yields a root which, ground up and dried, provides a fine porridge; while the marula fruit not only provides a liquor if it is pulped and allowed to ferment, but the pip is an edible nut with a high oil content.

The natural timber of Africa also fascinated Bvekenya with its commercial prospects. There were mahogany, ebony and a dozen other types of magnificent hardwood trees, growing side by side with innumerable varieties of their soft wooded brethren. Bvekenya had long nursed the project of obtaining control of some tract of the wilds, planting his selected trees in bulk, and leaving them to mature in their own environment with a minimum of care and expenditure.

While these projects of farming the produce of Africa matured in his mind, Bvekenya hunted as usual, and fortune was kind to him. In the 1928 hunting season alone he shot forty-five elephants. Their ivory was worth over £800, and his only difficulty in life was to smuggle the tusks and his whips to the market.

Each year he was being forced to improvise more cunning plans for smuggling. The old ivory trail through Punda Milia was now permanently closed. Most of his ivory had to be carried out on donkeys, straight through the bush between the Limpopo and Luvuvhu rivers. If he used a wagon, he always had to have a second empty vehicle travelling before it. If his advance guard of spies informed him that the police were approaching he would send the empty vehicle ahead to be searched, while the loaded vehicle would double in its tracks and pretend it was returning with provisions to the bush.

He was forced to exploit every opportunity for smuggling. Once Judge F. E.T. Krause came down with his wife and a party to visit the bush. Coetser, the ranger at Punda Milia asked Bvekenya to take them down to Pafuri in his tented wagon. Bvekenya was only too happy. Such a chance seldom occurred in those times.

Bvekenya took the party down to their chosen camping site in the trees on the banks of the Luvuvhu. Then he loaded 700 pounds of ivory on the wagon and sent it off "with the Judge's surplus camp kit" and to fetch supplies. Nobody searched it.

Not all of Bvekenya's devices worked quite so easily. He arranged once with a friend of his then stationed at Pafuri to send a load of ivory to market, along with a load from the recruiting organisation. Bvekenya had to meet the wagon between Pafuri and Punda Milia.

He took his ivory on donkeys down to the drift at Makhuleke. It was drizzling with rain and the river was in flood. Donkeys could always cross the river there, but this crossing was only practicable if the water was no higher than their stomachs.

On this day the river was too high for safety. There was a small canoe made of marula bark stationed at the place. In this craft Bvekenya ferried his ivory across. He stripped before he started and left his clothes in a hollow tree-trunk, in order to keep them dry.

Towards evening he finished ferrying the ivory across. It had been a laborious job. The Luvuvhu is a short river, but its floods are always violent. On this occasion the river had burst its banks and spread out far on either side, and finding a way in a boat through submerged reeds and bush was precarious.

Bvekenya went on to the rendezvous. He immediately saw from the tracks that the wagon had passed. The wagon men had not thought it possible that he would be able to cross in the flood, and accordingly they had travelled on.

Bvekenya returned to the river. It was getting dark and pouring with rain. It was too dark to return in the boat, and a school of hippos had arrived in his absence. They were splashing about in the reeds, grunting and bubbling, and there was nothing he could do to effect a passage.

He stood against a tree all night. It rained hard, but fortunately it was summer and the water was warm. The mosquitoes were the worst of his troubles. They almost ate him alive.

With the dawn, he ferried his ivory back across the river. By then the river had gone down somewhat and the hippos were dozing. He stored his ivory in a safe place and then made his way to the disused hut of Theodore Williams. There he drank a cup of quinine and a bottle of brandy and slept until the next morning.

The year 1929 started propitiously for Bvekenya. Hunting was good and elephants plentiful. For a change, he had gone down south of the Limpopo. The bush there was the intensely thick *nyanda* bush, too thick for any comfort in hunting; but for some reason many elephants were concentrated there that season.

His hunting was successful, but extremely arduous and dangerous in that dense tangle of trees and shrubs. He encountered one unusual elephant in these hunting grounds. Late one afternoon he found an elephant track and was surprised to see that the animal had four toes: one more than is usual in its kind.

Bvekenya followed the track. It led him into dense bush, about thirty miles south of the Limpopo. At sunset he found the animal. It was a fair-sized bull. He got in one shot, but the animal escaped. Bvekenya camped until dawn and then resumed the chase.

He soon came upon Four Toes. The elephant, in fact, found Bvekenya. Bvekenya's bullet had lodged in Four Toes' behind, and every time he had tried to relax he had grown more annoyed. He well knew that Bvekenya was following him. Elephants are sagacious creatures. If they sense a hunter on their trail they resort to extremes of cunning. They will walk back on their trail for miles, putting their feet in their own tracks, and will often walk in a circle to allow them to come up behind and find out who is following them.

Tracking an elephant, especially if he is wounded, is never easy; and there were many alarms. Four Toes led Bvekenya a weary chase. Then the animal's irritation overcame its prudence. It turned at bay in a clump of bush and laid an ambush. Bvekenya was a weary man when he approached the elephant, but he soon woke up.

Four Toes came out of his hiding place with a scream of rage. He crashed through the bush, leaving behind him the characteristic trail of a charging elephant: the ground marked as though a sledge had been pulled straight through the bush, with the tracks ominously blurred.

Bvekenya was an old hand at this game. He jumped to the side and slammed in two shots in a hurry as the elephant passed. Four Toes had a blast worse than his charge. He collapsed in a shower of sand and leaves and charged no more. His tusks were forty-five pounders, and Bvekenya cut the one foot off as a souvenir of a curious freak.

Another elephant oddity Bvekenya had shot some years before was an animal with three tusks. He had either been born like that, or at an early age had split one tusk so that it grew into twin units, side by side.

Bvekenya shot seven other elephants in the *nyanda* bush. All were wild, and three of them had previous bullet wounds. The area had obviously been hunted before by Portuguese or visiting hunters. He thought it discreet, therefore, to wander elsewhere, sending his £315 worth of ivory to Makhuleke as a precaution against any interference.

He was near the junction of the Olifants and Limpopo rivers when the Shanganes told him there were two big elephant bulls and a smaller animal in thin bush by the banks of a streamlet. They were grazing and taking life easy, and no hunter had tried to disturb them.

Bvekenya found the trio without any difficulty. The animals were scattered in the bush, grazing. The smaller elephant was nearest to him, and standing broadside on. Bvekenya selected his target and put a bullet accurately behind the shoulder.

There was a tremendous disturbance. The three elephants stampeded. Bvekenya had a momentary glimpse of the two larger animals. He sent a quick shot at one of them, but it seemed to have no effect. In the excitement he saw the third animal vanishing into the trees. It was an enormous bull. His heart pounded at the sight. He was certain it was Dhlulamithi.

The smaller elephant had run off with its companions. Suddenly it trumpeted wildly, skidded along the ground and dropped dead. Bvekenya left it to his Shanganes. He ran to Baba and mounted the horse. She was as thrilled as her master. She raced through the bush, past a stretch of lala palms and into some dwarf mupani.

The trail of Dhlulamithi was clear before him. The tracks were twenty-eight inches or more across. Bvekenya was wild with excitement. He could see the elephants ahead quite easily. They were stampeding straight for a Shangane village. Bvekenya felt a pang of alarm. There were no men in the village. He had stayed there the night before and he knew that the men were all at work.

He spurred Baba on. He raced up to within fifty yards of the elephants, but off to one side. There was no time to shoot. He could hear the women in the village screaming. He shouted at the elephants. They wheeled. The one darted off into the bush. Dhlulamithi put his trunk between his legs and came straight for Bvekenya.

Baba wheeled and fled like the wind. Bvekenya felt no fear. He was certain that his nimble little horse would outpace the elephant. Then the unexpected happened. The bush suddenly dwindled and they came upon the dried out floor of a lakelet. The mud of the floor was cracked, like the loose pieces of a huge jigsaw puzzle. The mud had dried hard, but the cracks were so wide that Baba put her feet into them as she ran. She had to slow down, and even then she tripped to her knees on several occasions.

Bvekenya glanced behind him. The elephant was still coming. The cracks presented no obstacle to his giant feet. Several times, when Baba tripped, Bvekenya felt the breath of death as the elephant trumpeted behind him. Each time Baba just scrambled up in time and dodged away.

At last they reached the edge of that nightmare lake. Baba tore up the slopes. There was a donga about six feet deep and almost twice that width before them. Baba took it in a leap and Bvekenya felt relieved. It would surely stop the elephant. He glanced behind him. Dhlulamithi was across the donga, but the crossing had delayed him. As Bvekenya looked, the elephant changed his course and crashed off into the bush. His temper had waned. Now he would run for miles to escape the menace of a hunter.

Bvekenya was determined to get the elephant. He collected Maribitane, one of his Shanganes, and set off on the trail, leaving his other followers to get the tusks of the fallen elephant.

It was a long chase. Many times before he had tracked an elephant for days on end, sleeping on the trail, eating nothing save berries or wild fruits, but never letting up.

They followed the trail of Dhlulamithi and his companion day after day. Every little detail of the trail was examined and interpreted. From the track of an elephant one can estimate even the length of time he has been before one. When the sun is hot the elephants will always rest a while in the shade. In the morning they will stand on the western side of the trees; after 11 a.m., when the sun is overhead, they will stand underneath the trees; while after 3 p.m. they will stand to the east, in order to find the shade.

With this knowledge, the hunter will know roughly how many hours ahead the animals are. The condition of the branches they have broken and the dryness of their droppings will indicate whether they are days ahead.

If they travel in the night, the dew falls and their feet become wet. The sand sticks to their feet and the track becomes blurred. If they walk in the day the dew is dry and the track is clear and crisp in the sand.

Elephants leave many other signs. If they lie down the hunter can judge the length of their tusks. If the tusks are small their points will dig into the ground. If the tusks are long the hunter will see the mark of their curve.

The size of the track is never an indication of the length of the tusks, and is not even reliable as a guide to the height of the animal. In a good season the foot fattens out; in a drought it may shrink; and a cow feeding a calf always loses condition.

From the ivory hunter's point of view, even a big elephant may be valueless. Bvekenya had trailed one animal once with an impressive track. After a weary chase he eventually shot it in the midst of the bush and found the elephant to be a freak, without any sign of a tusk.

Of the tusks of Dhlulamithi, however, there was no doubt. Day followed day as they trailed the elephants northwards. During the nights they slept in a crude camp, eating such food as Maribitane had been able to find in the bush.

The were both weary of the chase.

"They are big elephants," said Maribitane one night, "but we travel far. Must we walk our feet into ruin just because of these elephants?"

"For long I have wanted this one big elephant," Bvekenya said gruffly. "I would give much to shoot him, and to find that Folage."

Maribitane looked at him curiously.

"Sir," he said, "you are like a man who has all and yet dies for want of the stars and the moon. That Folage is old now, if not dead. You took his eye in payment for that fight. He paid a great price for the things he did. He is nothing save a broken police-boy, if he still lives. You are Bvekenya. You ruined him. What more do you want? Must hatred live forever with you, as it does with bandits in the bush? This elephant. You have shot many. You have shot your three hundred and more; and once you said you would be content with that. Now it is always more."

"Shut up," said Bvekenya. He rolled over and tried to sleep. But he was neither certain of himself nor content. Thoughts crowded in upon him. Must he roam forever? He had even dabbled with the idea of trying fresh hunting grounds in far-off Kenya. But this would only postpone the inevitable decision; to remain in the wilderness and continue to kill, or take himself home and create something good? He worried through the night. When he drowsed he saw his father, now over eighty years of age, and all alone upon his farm. Then Bvekenya slept.

The next afternoon they found the elephants. They came upon them in a small valley of mupani trees. The elephants were quite unaware of them. While Bvekenya and his Shangane watched them through the trees, the smaller turned and walked towards them. In another minute he would see them. Bvekenya lifted his gun and fired. He aimed at Dhlulamithi in the distance. There was a smack as the bullet connected. He took a second quick shot at the nearest elephant. Both elephants wheeled and ran into the bush. Bvekenya reloaded as he ran to the right, trying to get below a slight east wind.

He stopped and listened. There was no sound. He scrambled up an old mupani tree and searched the countryside. He saw nothing. Some sound made him look down.

He saw the two elephants, one behind the other, coming very fast towards his tree. They both had their trunks up, sniffing, and seemed very surprised at what had happened.

Bvekenya was only about ten feet up, and the elephants were nearing his tree. He caught hold of a branch above him to scramble higher. While he pulled himself up, the branch he had just left broke off as the leading elephant brushed against it.

Bvekenya lifted himself still higher. He raised his head to the next branch. He looked into the eyes of death. There were two green mambas coiled up lovingly on the bough, and neither of them looked as though they liked the disturbance.

"God," said Bvekenya. Better the elephants than those horrors. He dropped down through the leaves. He landed on the hindquarters of Dhlulamithi. His gun slipped off on one side of the elephant and he fell to the ground on the other. He twisted in the air and landed on his feet. He ran for his life, but he might just as well have walked. The elephants rushed on without heed into the bush of the north.

Maribitane ran up to him.

"Why did you let go?" he asked.

Bvekenya told him of the snakes. He clapped his hands in wonder.

"Your time is drawing to an end here in the bush."

Bvekenya was despondent. He went and retrieved the gun. They cleaned it of sand and followed the elephants. Five miles further on they came across the smaller animal. From his trail they could see that he was walking sideways. He must have been wounded, although there was no blood. He was standing in a clearing, sniffing and tossing sand into the air to see which way the wind was blowing.

For him, it was an ill wind whichever way it blew.

Bvekenya put five bullets into him. He fell to the ground with a sigh. There was no sign or sound of Dhlulamithi.

They camped and feasted on the elephant that night. Both men were famished, and half silly with tiredness.

"What is to be the end of you?" asked Maribitane, looking at Bvekenya over the fire. "I was only a youngster when you first came, now I have children. Will you always live like this? Will you hunt till you die? Then will the police make us account for your life? Will it always be just one more elephant?"

Bvekenya brushed him off. He tried to sleep. Instead, he had nightmares about the two snakes. He dreamed his gun turned into a mamba when he touched it.

With dawn his other two Shanganes, Sebeyane and Kommetje, arrived with the donkeys. They had been following the hunters' trail. They were left to cut the tusks out, while Bvekenya and Maribitane went on after Dhlulamithi. For two more days they tracked the elephant. Their feet were sore and their clothes in rags. They were covered in dust and grime.

They found Dhlulamithi at last, standing wearily in the shade of a tall thombothi tree. Bvekenya studied him long and silently. He stalked the elephant slowly and skilfully. He found his range and his ideal target. The elephant seemed weary and heedless. Bvekenya lifted his gun. He found his favourite shot: the most deadly mark of all. He could hear Maribitane breathing jerkily beside him, waiting for the kill.

He saw the elephant's eyes: its weatherbeaten face, the wrinkles in its skin, the tremors of its body, the waving of its ears with the ragged ends where the thorns had torn them. He saw the scars of ancient battles and the slight wound of his own bullet. He saw the elephant in its strength and its wisdom, its savagery, patience and courage. He saw Africa, and he knew that he loved it.

He put down the gun.

"Let him live," he said, while Maribitane stared at him in wonder. "I have had my day. That witch was right. I must grow taller than these trees, else I shall die in their midst like a wild animal, an outcast from my own kind. I have killed enough. He will live on in the bush. His cows will give him fine sons, strong bulls with great tusks. They will make up for those I have slaughtered."

So he went his way. It was November, 1929. To each of his hunters, and those who had become his friends or dependants, he gave money and cattle to keep them for life. Then he went westwards to Crooks Corner for the last time; and in the broad Limpopo waters he washed the dust of the wilderness from his feet for good. He went off to his farm on the plains. He married Maria Badenhorst, who had loved him for long, and with her raised four fine sons and a pretty daughter.

As for Dhlulamithi, he went his way through the trees and the bush, the flats and the desert. And truly, his cows gave him the strong sons Bvekenya had wished him.

Today there are more elephants in that wilderness than in Bvekenya's time. Still does the forest live and the great rivers run with their teeming animal life. Still do the Shanganes speak of Bvekenya, his deeds and his ways and the manner of his passing. Still do they hope that some day he may return; and maybe he will, but only at death, when spirits wander off and a hunter's soul follows the Ivory Trail in the tracks of Dhlulamithi.

Bvekenya died on 2 June 1962, in his bed on his farm Vlakplaas, near Geysdorp in the Western Transvaal.